Praise for *The Financial Impact Negotiation*

'Better than any other I've seen, this book identifies the psychological factors underlying each of the major stages of the negotiation process and describes how to harness them for success.'

Dr Robert Cialdini, Author of *Influence* and *Pre-Suasion*

'All negotiation practitioners need to read this essential book by the talented and insightful Prof. Dr Kasia Jagodzinska. She methodically outlines the critical steps from preparation to agreement through sustaining implementation. Most importantly, she highlights the emotional factors always present in any high-stakes negotiation. A must read.'

Gary Noesner, Chief, FBI Crisis Negotiation Unit (retired)

'Dr Jagodzinska walks the negotiator through the entire process of high impact negotiations and the many challenges that will arise during the complex process, starting with understanding yourself first. This book is an essential guide for any business negotiator.'

Lieutenant Jack Cambria, Instructor, Police Advisor, Corporate Trainer, NYPD Hostage Team Commander, USA

'This book offers an excellent overview of the challenging process of negotiation and is a must read for all those actively involved in business.'

Jonathan Faust, SVP/Global Controller, HP Inc., USA

'This is a fantastic brain teaser and compendium guiding you through the complete high-impact negotiation process. You might find insights which turn your long-standing practices up-side-down. . . only to become an even better negotiator.'

Anette Weber, Management Board Member and Group CFO, Bucherer AG, Switzerland

'The book takes the reader through the negotiation process from start to finish and is filled with practical tools and approaches to help you become a winning negotiator. Beginner or negotiation expert, all will find concrete tips and advice ready for immediate use in this great guide.'

René Koets, Partner, Head of Management Consulting,
KPMG Switzerland

THE FINANCIAL TIMES GUIDE TO HIGH-IMPACT NEGOTIATION

Pearson

At Pearson, we believe in learning – all kinds of learning for all kinds of people. Whether it's at home, in the classroom or in the workplace, learning is the key to improving our life chances.

That's why we're working with leading authors to bring you the latest thinking and best practices, so you can get better at the things that are important to you. You can learn on the page or on the move, and with content that's always crafted to help you understand quickly and apply what you've learned.

If you want to upgrade your personal skills or accelerate your career, become a more effective leader or more powerful communicator, discover new opportunities or simply find more inspiration, we can help you make progress in your work and life.

Every day our work helps learning flourish, and wherever learning flourishes, so do people.

To learn more, please visit us at **www.pearson.com/uk**

The Financial Times

With a worldwide network of highly respected journalists, *The Financial Times* provides global business news, insightful opinion and expert analysis of business, finance and politics. With over 500 journalists reporting from 50 countries worldwide, our in-depth coverage of international news is objectively reported and analysed from an independent, global perspective.

To find out more, visit **www.ft.com**

THE FINANCIAL TIMES GUIDE TO HIGH-IMPACT NEGOTIATION

A COMPREHENSIVE GUIDE FOR EXECUTING VALUABLE DEALS AND PARTNERSHIPS

DR KASIA JAGODZINSKA

 Pearson

Harlow, England • London • New York • Boston • San Francisco • Toronto • Sydney
Dubai • Singapore • Hong Kong • Tokyo • Seoul • Taipei • New Delhi
Cape Town • São Paulo • Mexico City • Madrid • Amsterdam • Munich • Paris • Milan

PEARSON EDUCATION LIMITED
KAO Two
KAO Park
Harlow CM17 9NA
United Kingdom
Tel: +44 (0)1279 623623
Web: www.pearson.com/uk

First edition published 2023 (print and electronic)

ISBN: 978-1-292-40038-9 (print)
       978-1-292-40040-2 (PDF)
       978-1-292-40039-6 (ePub)

British Library Cataloguing-in-Publication Data
A catalogue record for the print edition is available from the British Library

Library of Congress Cataloging-in-Publication Data
Names: Jagodzinska, Kasia, author.
Title: The Financial Times guide to high impact negotiation / Kasia
    Jagodzinska.
Other titles: Guide to high impact negotiation
Description: First Edition. | Hoboken, NJ : Pearson Education, 2023. |
    Includes bibliographical references and index.
Identifiers: LCCN 2022042300 | ISBN 9781292400389 (hardcover) | ISBN
    9781292400396 (epub) | ISBN 9781292400402 (pdf)
Subjects: LCSH: Negotiation in business.
Classification: LCC HD58.6 .J34 2023 | DDC 658.4/052--dc23/eng/20220909
LC record available at https://lccn.loc.gov/2022042300

10 9 8 7 6 5 4 3 2 1
26 25 24 23 22

Cover design by Michelle Morgan, At the Pop Ltd
Front cover image Peshkova/Shutterstock

Print edition typeset in Stone Serif ITC Pro 9.5/14 by Straive
Printed by Ashford Colour Press Ltd, Gosport

NOTE THAT ANY PAGE CROSS REFERENCES REFER TO THE PRINT EDITION

For my parents, with eternal love

CONTENTS

Pearson's Commitment to Diversity, Equity and Inclusion

Pearson is dedicated to creating bias-free content that reflects the diversity, depth and breadth of all learners' lived experiences. We embrace the many dimensions of diversity including, but not limited to, race, ethnicity, gender, sex, sexual orientation, socioeconomic status, ability, age and religious or political beliefs.

Education is a powerful force for equity and change in our world. It has the potential to deliver opportunities that improve lives and enable economic mobility. As we work with authors to create content for every product and service, we acknowledge our responsibility to demonstrate inclusivity and incorporate diverse scholarship so that everyone can achieve their potential through learning. As the world's leading learning company, we have a duty to help drive change and live up to our purpose to help more people create a better life for themselves and to create a better world.

Our ambition is to purposefully contribute to a world where:

- Everyone has an equitable and lifelong opportunity to succeed through learning.
- Our educational products and services are inclusive and represent the rich diversity of learners.
- Our educational content accurately reflects the histories and lived experiences of the learners we serve.
- Our educational content prompts deeper discussions with students and motivates them to expand their own learning and worldview.

We are also committed to providing products that are fully accessible to all learners. As per Pearson's guidelines for accessible educational Web media, we test and retest the capabilities of our products against the highest standards for every release, following the WCAG guidelines in developing new products for copyright year 2022 and beyond. You can learn more about Pearson's commitment to accessibility at:

https://www.pearson.com/us/accessibility.html

While we work hard to present unbiased, fully accessible content, we want to hear from you about any concerns or needs regarding this Pearson product so that we can investigate and address them.

- Please contact us with concerns about any potential bias at:
  https://www.pearson.com/report-bias.html

- For accessibility-related issues, such as using assistive technology with Pearson products, alternative text requests, or accessibility documentation, email the Pearson Disability Support team at:
  disability.support@pearson.com

AUTHOR'S ACKNOWLEDGEMENTS

The greatest blessing for an author is to be surrounded by people that inspire, challenge, support and push you to do better. Working on this book was an opportunity to meet many wonderful professionals who graciously agreed to share their experiences with me and my readers. As I go through the list of names that I jotted down, the story of creation replays. Each interview left a specific impression and made an imprint in my mind and in the pages of this book.

I would like to thank Eloise Cook, my publisher from Pearson, for her highly professional support and excellent guidance that made for a smooth writing process.

I am forever grateful to Mike for his constant motivation and pushing me to go beyond my own limitations and for his unwavering faith in me. You are and always were my strength.

Honorary Professor Michel Maciej Kostecki was my intellectual and emotional companion throughout this journey, and so many others. I am happy I took that seat next to you on the plane over Paris years ago. Meeting you changed the course of my life, for which I cannot begin to express my gratitude.

It is precious to be able to rely on someone. Thank you to Marcin for being there for me. Our best talks on business and life were in the middle of the Aegean Sea.

I would also like to thank my training participants, clients and students for opening up and sharing your challenges with me. It is because of you that I see the purpose of my work.

The interviews with renowned experts have been crucial to the development of this book. First and foremost, I would like to express my gratitude to FBI Agent Gary Noesner. You are indeed the most likeable, generous and professional person I have ever met. I am thankful for our meeting, which gave the start to an enriching and valuable friendship.

I feel privileged to have met Lieutenant Jack Cambria, a true gentleman. NYPD was lucky to have you. Thank you for being extremely responsive and offering me as much time as I needed to learn from you.

I have always valued people who walk the talk. I wish to express my gratitude to the legendary Dr Robert Cialdini for an insightful interview with a personal touch. The principle of similarity with the reference you made to Wroclaw was much appreciated.

René Koets, you were the first interviewee and thanks to you I kicked off the process with a great vibe. Your professionalism and charisma shine through your words.

The interview with Alexander Kostecki was a mental game-changer. Thank you for your refreshing and visionary views on negotiation, with a truly New York vibe at its best.

Thank you to Anette Weber for a very straightforward and friendly interview. Your advice about healthy habits helped me get back on track when the writing process was becoming overly consuming.

We seldom encounter high-profile professionals quoting Shakespeare with reference to business. Thank you, Sonalee Parekh for a mind-opening, sophisticated and open interview. The exchange with you was an intellectual treat.

Sometimes the people we meet, even if briefly, instantly become our role models. Meeting Michèle Ollier was one of such experiences for me. Thank you for your sophistication and professional approach.

Among the many inspiring women who I met was Tania Micki to whom I am grateful for her support and sharing her proficient approach to negotiations, in the professional sphere and beyond.

It takes real expertise to be able to afford to be spontaneous. Benita Hess pulled it off with great ease. Thank you for our unprompted interview and an eye for new opportunities.

Fabienne Schlup-Hasselmann, your beautiful soul and wisdom shone through the interview. Thank you for your professionalism with a human touch. I wish we had more businesswomen like you.

I would like to thank Jonathan Faust for a friendly and extremely efficient interview. I value your unconventional outlook on negotiations, in business and beyond. This is what makes you so successful.

I am grateful to Sean Whitley Very for sharing great tips on closing deals. Thank you for being extremely responsive and efficient with setting up and executing the interview. We need more business professionals like you!

Thank you Dr Daniel Schönfelder for being a man of your word. I appreciate that you found the time to do the promised interview months after successfully concluding one of your many high-impact negotiations. It was great to draw inspiration from your experiences.

My gratitude goes out to Dan Staner for entrusting me with the development of his teams. Thank you for the free-flowing interview in Verbier. The best ideas flourish when one is surrounded by great people and a nice setting.

The interview with Dr Stephan Hartmann was a practical application of negotiation skills. Thank you for your meticulous preparation and sharing your well thought-through ideas.

I also wish to thank Alessandro Soldati for being extremely responsive and for providing refreshing insights on negotiating in high-potential start-ups.

I wish to include Krystyna and Krzysztof Stepinscy among the people who supported me during the writing process. The life and business anecdotes you shared were a source of inspiration. I will never forget the special moments our families spent together.

This book is dedicated to my parents. Thank you for everything. For all the sacrifices you made so that I can live a better life and enjoy what I do, among others being able to write books. No acknowledgements can do justice to my feelings and gratitude for you.

PUBLISHER'S ACKNOWLEDGEMENTS

Text Credits:

3 **Henry Ford:** Quote by Henry Ford; 5 **Diane Warren:** If I Could Turn Back Time lyrics © Diane Warren; 12 **Dr Robert Cialdini:** Interview with Dr Robert Cialdini; 14 **The Finanical Times Ltd:** Hill, A. Negotiation is tough and should be left to professionals. *Financial Times*, January 20, 2020. © The Financial Times Limited 2020. All Rights Reserved; 17 **Lewis Carroll:** Lewis Carroll, Alice in Wonderland; 18 **Abraham Lincoln:** Quote by Abraham Lincoln; 25 **René Koets:** Interview with René Koets; 29 **Russel L. Honoré:** Quote by Russel L. Honoré; 38 **Tania Micki:** Interview of Tania Micki; 41 **Richelle E. Goodrich:** Quote by Richelle E. Goodrich; 45 **Jonathan Faust:** Interview of Jonathan Faust; 51 **Idries Shah:** Quote by Idries Shah; 53 **Michèle Ollier:** Interview of Michèle Ollier; 61 **The Finanical Times Ltd:** Ku, Gillian. Negotiation skills: time to ditch the winner-takes-all approach. *Financial Times*, March 28, 2017. © The Financial Times Limited 2017. All Rights Reserved; 65 **Jim Rohn:** Quote by Jim Rohn; 73 **Business Expert Press:** Adopted from K. Jagodzinska, *Negotiation Booster: The Ultimate Self-Empowerment Guide to High Impact Negotiations*, Business Expert Press, New York, 2020.; 74 **Dr Stephan Hartmann:** Interview of Dr Stephan Hartmann; 76 **The Finanical Times Ltd:** Harford, T. Compromise dies in the age of outrage. *Financial Times*, May 31, 2019. © The Financial Times Limited 2019. All Rights Reserved; 79 **Kristin Armstrong:** Quote by Kristin Armstrong; 87 **Fabienne Schlup-Hasselmann:** Interview of Fabienne Schlup-Hasselmann; 93 **Lord Byron:** Don Juan: By Lord Byron, Volume 1; 99 **Sonalee Parekh:** Interview of Sonalee Parekh; 115 **Jack Cambria:** Interview of Lieutenant Jack Cambria; 117 **John C. Maxwell:** Quote by John Maxwell; 118 **Samuel Butler:** Quote by Samuel Butler; 120 **Benita Hess:** Interview of Benita Hess; 123 **Alessandro Soldati:** Interview of Alessandro Soldati; 131 **Karl Albrecht:** Quote by Karl Albrecht; 137 **Dan Staner:** Interview of Dan Staner; 140 **Anette Weber:** Interview of Anette Weber;

143 Henry David Thoreau: Quote by Henry David Thoreau; **154 Alexander Kostecki:** Interview of Alexander Kostecki; **157 William Shakespeare:** A quote from William Shakespeare's, *A Midsummer Night's Dream Act 1 Scene 1*; **162 Dr Daniel Schönfelder:** Interview of Dr Daniel Schönfelder; **164 Sean Whitley:** Interview of Sean Whitley; **167 Johann Wolfgang Von Goethe:** Quote by Johann Wolfgang Von Goethe; **173 Gary Noesner:** Interview of Gary Noesner; **185 Business Expert Press:** Adapted from Negotiation Booster.

Photo Credit:

FM BIG studio: Used with Permission from BIG studio.

ABOUT THE AUTHOR

Prof. Dr Kasia Jagodzinska combines an academic career with international business practice in the field of negotiations. In her role of international negotiation expert, she coaches and trains executives from the biggest corporations in Europe, the US, Asia and the Middle East, such as Moderna, Microsoft, KPMG, Amazon, Adobe, HPE (Hewlett Packard Enterprise), Tecan, BASF and others.

Drawing from her training in Jungian analytical psychology, she incorporates the dynamics of power, the ego factor and the awareness of psychological factors into her training sessions.

She served as a senior adviser to the United Nations in Geneva, where her mission was to provide assistance in multi-stakeholder negotiations and conflict of interest management.

As a professor, she works with students from universities in Switzerland, France, Italy and Poland. She holds a PhD in International Law, is multilingual and multicultural, having lived and worked in several countries.

Dr Jagodzinska is the founder of Negotiation Booster (www.negotiationbooster. com), an innovative approach to business negotiations that leverages the task-related aspects of a negotiation with the underlying psychological factors. This new methodology is captured in two of her books. In *Negotiation Booster: The Ultimate Self-Empowerment Guide to High-Impact Negotiations* (Business Expert Press, 2020) she shares strategies for thriving in negotiations by means of directional self-management. *Negotiate Your Way to Success: Personal Guidelines to Boost Your Career* (Business Expert Press, 2021) is a collection of pragmatic guidelines flowing from the situations, both good and bad, that she experienced negotiating across the globe.

Working with business professionals from various industries and sectors gave her an in-depth understanding of the challenges they face in their high-impact negotiations. Empowering others to succeed and boosting their negotiation power is her passion.

INTRODUCTION

The Financial Times Guide to High-Impact Negotiation is a comprehensive framework for winning negotiations. It guides the reader through the complete process of negotiation: from preparation and dealing to closing and implementing the negotiated terms. The time you invest in reading this book will allow you to avoid the common pitfalls associated with high-impact negotiations. This book will serve as your strategic guide to your bargaining excellence. Imagine the pay-off for your future negotiations and the competitive advantage this will provide you with.

Strategic preparation, execution and success in high-impact negotiations are very much a cause-and-effect equation. The simple reason is that a negotiator who enters a negotiation with a clear understanding of the objective and a step-by-step guide on how to reach that objective is governed by reason rather than emotions. Internally this allows for a focused execution of the negotiation strategy; externally it is perceived as a sign of confidence, strength of the negotiation team and power – the marks of business success.

Many negotiators fail because they allow emotions, lack of clarity and strategic confusion to cloud the negotiation process. Often the simple act of labelling a negotiation as 'difficult' or 'high stakes' is enough to throw some negotiators off the rationality cliff and jeopardise the chances of reaching agreements or compromise their company goals.

> *If I had eight hours to chop down a tree, I'd spend six sharpening my axe* (A. Lincoln).

Contrary to this saying, often negotiations are approached in an intuitive, haphazard manner. Negotiators tend to operate based on certain ingrained habits that they have created throughout the years of their business activities. As a result, internal company negotiations are often a mosaic of habitual patterns of the involved individuals. The negotiation team has no unified approach and there is no clear negotiation mission. This lack of internal alignment is then transplanted to external negotiations. There is no negotiation task force nor a clear executive plan. This is especially risky in high-impact deals. To mitigate this risk, the members involved in high-value deals need a roadmap on how to prepare strategically, what negotiating processes to implement and execute, and how to avoid pitfalls in order to reach the best deal.

Negotiation, like any other business endeavour, has a monetary value. However, in high-impact deals this value often exceeds the amount of the deal itself. Company goodwill, branding, long-term business opportunities and professional relationships are at stake. Understanding the negotiation process and preparing for it from a strategic perspective is the ultimate form of business management. A unified negotiation mission reflected in the adopted strategy allows the negotiator to come across professionally, to be seen as a trusted business partner and to fulfil the organisational objectives.

A negotiation does not end with a deal being signed. It is concluded when the negotiated terms are implemented and there is a solid business relationship between the parties. Getting this logic right is what differentiates deal-makers from real-makers. The former have a high volume of signed paperwork, which does not necessarily translate into long-lasting and executable agreements. A real-maker is a negotiator who has the ability to seize untapped business opportunities by bridging the execution of the task while strengthening the relationship in the long term. In order to become a real-maker, the negotiator needs to understand how to strategically prepare, execute the process and align it with the company goals.

The Financial Times Guide to High-Impact Negotiation is for anyone who is required to negotiate and who needs a strategic, easy-to-follow guide to the process. It bridges tactical preparation with self-management. This combination allows you to develop a negotiation mindset characterised by an elevated level of self-control, confidence and bargaining power. This approach impacts all the members of the negotiation team. It reflects the negotiation mission and values of the company. A successful collective mindset based on strategic fundaments attracts further success in the business arena and beyond.

How this book works

This guide equips you with a straightforward and user-friendly framework. This can be used to prepare for a negotiation or as a reference guide at any time during a negotiation to boost your chances of reaching executable high-impact agreements while securing longevity of the business relationship. The book introduces a strategic approach to the negotiation process: concrete steps that need to be taken to put the negotiation plan into actions that help accomplish the negotiation mission, reach the task-oriented goals and fulfil the business relationship objective. The presented outlook leverages executive thinking and acting to ensure long-term competitiveness through negotiation agility.

This book provides you with a holistic guide to negotiation. Consequently, it is divided into two parts. The first part introduces the negotiation mindset necessary for strategic preparation. You will discover how to define the nego-tiation mission statement, what things to take into account when you set the goal, how to define the objective, which information to gather, how to choose the right approach and what to pay attention to when negotiating virtually. The second part focuses on the negotiation process. In this part you will learn how to design the right environment for creating value in negotiations. You will explore how to take the lead in the negotiation by opening the discussion and successfully executing the dealing phase. The final step on the negotiation journey is closing the deal and keeping the dynamic alive after the negotiation.

The Financial Times Guide to High-Impact Negotiation is a goldmine of practical insights flowing from:

- The author's experiences working with high-profile negotiators, business professionals, EU and UN officials from across the globe.
- Interviews with world-renowned negotiators and experts who share their practical expertise including:
  - Agent Gary Noesner from the Federal Bureau of Investigation (FBI) Crisis Negotiation Unit;
  - Lieutenant Jack Cambria from the New York City Police Department's (NYPD) Hostage Negotiation Team;
  - Dr Robert Cialdini, author, keynote speaker and renowned scientist in the study of influence.
- Interviews with leading business and industry experts from: BASF, Bucherer, Cartier, Clair, Goldavenue, HP Inc., KPMG, Medicxi, Mitto, Moderna, RingCentral, Roland Berger, Tecan.

Furthermore, each chapter equips you with hands-on features that will enable you to put the theory into practice and to apply the concepts to your specific negotiation context. The tools consist of:

- templates and checklists to help you plan your negotiation from start to finish;
- real-life examples that highlight the most common pitfalls made by negotiators and practical tips on how to avoid them;
- exercises for self-practice;
- self-assessment tools for evaluating and monitoring your progress;
- articles from *The Financial Times* to get you thinking.

PART 1
THE NEGOTIATION MINDSET

CHAPTER 1
NEGOTIATION STARTS FROM WITHIN

'Whether you think you can or think you can't, you're right.'

Henry Ford

What you will discover in this chapter:

- The most common challenges that professionals face in negotiations and how to overcome them
- How to persuade your own mind to increase your negotiation power
- Practical techniques for self-empowerment

Manage yourself before you jump into the negotiation process

Negotiation is not only a transactional exchange between two people. In the era of B2B, B2C, C2C and C2B business models it is easy to forget that a negotiation cannot be locked into an acronym. If it could, the best bet would be H2H – human to human. Negotiation is primarily an interaction between two people with their needs, fears, preoccupations, hopes and aspirations. First and foremost, it begins with you. For this reason, we will start our journey with the mindset and then move on with the process design. In high-pressure negotiations, put your own oxygen mask on first before you engage in interpersonal dynamics and jump into the process. A lot of work can be done on the internal level to increase your bargaining power. A good place to start is by looking at the universally shared challenges. The realisation that you are not alone is in itself comforting.

In real-life negotiations, many feel like they need to put on an act. The label of negotiator calls for supporting behaviours. Being tough is often the default mode. Its result is usually a power-based negotiation approach. In reality, the tough act can be a cover for inner insecurities. After all, the best defence is attack. Or is it? Skilled negotiators don't need to pretend, because they feel empowered. They rely on their inner confidence and combine it with strategic preparation and design of the process.

Negotiation training is a privileged space. It is there that masks come off and professionals feel comfortable enough to openly share the difficulties that they face in their daily negotiations. The years I spent training, consulting and assisting business professionals in their negotiation journey have shown me that the pool of challenges that they face is universal: they start from within. A successful negotiation begins with self-management: taking control of your emotions, fears, ego, existing habits, biases and beliefs. **The first and most important negotiator you need to win over is yourself.**

My training sessions usually start with a round table of introductions where I ask the participants to say a few words about themselves and share their most challenging negotiation situation. Two things become apparent. The first one is related to the structure of these introductory rounds. The person who starts sets the tone and the framework. For example, if they say their name, their role, number of years in the company and mention something about their private life, the person who goes next follows the exact same pattern. I have never seen a variation from this. This is a crucial lesson for real-life negotiations. **Be the one who starts the negotiation process by informally designing the scene; others will follow in your footsteps.** Negotiation is not a race and is not to be treated as such. It does not start when the starting pistol is fired. It commences when the two negotiators first meet. The way they build the interpersonal relation from the beginning can make the process much easier going forward. **Work the person first, then the case.**

The second observation is the attention with which the participants listen to others who are sharing their experiences. It is eye-opening for them to realise that they are not alone in their dilemmas. The chances are that if others in the meeting have similar experiences, so will their negotiation partner. At my end I can testify to that. It has happened that both parties on opposite sides of the table have confided in me. Their preoccupations were indeed pretty much the same.

The most common challenges and how to overcome them: insights from Cher and psychiatrists from Madagascar

Awareness is the first step to change. Being aware of your personal challenges will help you increase your confidence and performance in the negotiation. Here is a simple and quick technique to identify the main negotiation habit that is holding you back from your full potential. You might be familiar with the song by the singer Cher: 'If I could turn back time'. This is exactly what you should do mentally. After each negotiation, big or small, ask yourself one question: *If I could turn back time, what would I do differently?* Do this personal debrief ten times and you will notice a pattern of behaviour. You will spot the same mistake in a different guise. Once you identify it, you can replace it with desired actions.

The primary challenge that business professionals have shared with me is related to self-empowerment; all other difficulties stem from this one. It is worthwhile to examine the concept of power. In the classic, externally oriented outlook, power is the capacity for person A to get person B to do what person B would not have done without the intervention of person A. According to another definition, power is the capacity to act to obtain desired outcomes and reach certain objectives. This dimension is intrinsic, which means that power is an inner resource and it can be unleashed both internally and externally. The good news is that there are techniques on how to do this.

An interesting technique of self-empowerment comes from certain accounts of dynamic psychiatry from Madagascar. It is called *the Bilo.* The word designates a technique used to cure patients suffering from low self-esteem. It involves a ritual. Over a period of 15 days, the low self-esteem individual takes on the role of a king and is treated as such. All the people in his surrounding dress and act like servants in his court. They address him as 'King', treat him with the utmost respect, prepare feasts and dances for him. On the last day, the 'coronation' takes place. The 'King' is dressed in festive attire and mounts on a platform of about two and a half meters with a small statue at his feet. From the elevated space, he dines while the court performs a sacrifice for them. Most patients come down miraculously liberated from their previous low self-esteem. I am not suggesting you perform the whole ritual but it might help if you surround yourself with people that can boost your self-esteem and treat you as a strong negotiator. Eventually, you will start seeing yourself as such.

Here are some comments that point towards lack of belief in one's power from modern business professionals.

- It is difficult to advance my position and to see myself as a valid player.
- I believe I am not a natural negotiator. If the discussion gets more emotional/personal, I perform worse as a negotiator on the strategic level.
- I engage in reactive behaviour and allow myself to be governed by emotions.
- I do not have the conviction that I am in the power seat.
- I do not feel confident that I can succeed.
- I see the other party as 'difficult' and myself as weak.
- I struggle to find a balance between reason and emotions.
- I doubt that I have a voice in the negotiation.

Do you see a reflection of yourself in any of these examples? If so, you might benefit from the following self-negotiation technique. Its aim is to help you proactively prepare by balancing a strategic approach with psychological reinforcement. This combination is powerful in unblocking the sensation that *you* have an impact on the process and releasing your inner bargaining power.

Interrogative self-negotiation technique

Step 1: Can I move this person?
How to do this: Create an environment where both you and the other party need something from each other. Identify what their needs might be and how only you can fulfil them. Be open-minded and creative. Do not negotiate down with yourself. Do not be over-critical.

Step 2: Answer in writing
How to do this: Take a piece of paper and write down all the assets you possess that might be valuable to the other party. This will visually show you how many things you have going on for you that you might not be fully aware of. Keep the list in sight to stay motivated.

Step 3: List three specific reasons why your answer is 'yes'
How to do this: Focus on the positives. Create scenarios with a 'sky is the limit' mindset. Be clear and precise. Avoid wishful thinking (it would be great if, If only they would). Instead use the formula: They will accept my proposal, because. . . .

▶

Step 4: How will you design the process?

How to do this: Think about how you will prepare, how you will open the negotiation, what demands you will bring to the table, which strategies and tactics you will apply. You will discover this in more detail throughout this book; alternatively you can refer to the table of contents, which has been designed to serve as a blueprint framework.

Step 5: How will you manage yourself?

How to do this: Which technique of self-empowerment discussed in this chapter resonates with you most? Use it as your default self-empowerment boost.

The secondary challenges negotiators face fall into three main categories: emotions-management, confidence-related and strategic.

Emotions-management challenges

The following are a few examples of emotional challenges that negotiators encounter.

- Dealing with an emotional counterpart impacts them personally.
- They hate conflict and will do everything to avoid it.
- Trigger causes their emotional outburst.
- They succumb to emotional manipulation and pressure.
- Empathy makes them more sensitive.

Although we would like to think we are the rational kind, humans are primarily governed by feelings. Since negotiation is a H2H interaction, two emotional energies collide. If handled without caution, this can negatively affect the ongoing negotiation. For example, you can get personally affected by what your negotiating partner says or does. The best approach is to never take things personally. Remind yourself that the other party also has their challenges, vulnerabilities and shortcomings. This will make it easier for you to focus your energy on the objective you are trying to achieve.

You might be wondering what you could possibly do to have fewer emotional reactions during a negotiation. As much as negotiations are an H2H encounter, there must be a strategic framework for the process. You can be passionate about what you are negotiating; however, the moment you start negotiating, reason must take control over feelings. If not, a skilled negotiating partner can benefit from your inner emotional battles.

If you notice that your feelings are starting to affect your judgement and your reactions, you can ask to take a break. There is nothing wrong in wanting to take a breather and use this time to refocus on the objective you set for this negotiation. You can use this technique whether you have been emotionally triggered by something which was said, or you realise that what you are saying is no longer rational. The most important point is to know when to take a step back and compose yourself (the turn-back time exercise might prove helpful).

How to overcome emotions-management challenges: Chessboard technique

Close your eyes and imagine that your negotiation situation is a chessboard. The circumstances are the board and the players are the pawns. It is vital that you imagine the negotiation landscape in every single detail. Make the situation as real as possible in your mind. How would you behave and how would you like to see your negotiation partner acting? Where would the interaction be taking place? What would be the setting? How powerful and optimistic would you be feeling?

Now go one step further. Imagine that you are the 'hand of God', that you have the power to move the pawns. How would you design the chessboard to achieve your objectives? To conclude, visualise the movement of the pawns that brings you to a negotiation checkmate.

An alternative method is **mental rehearsal.**

This is how it works. Close your eyes. Repeatedly imagine you are successfully negotiating, for example opening the negotiation from a position of power, bringing in demands with conviction, closing the deal, leading the discussion in a constructive manner, and so on. Mentally construct the future outcome you want. Remind yourself of the challenges you want to let go of and replace them by who you want to be. Think about your future actions. Plan the desired choices and rehearse performing the successful action until it feels like part of your new reality.

Confidence-related challenges

The following are a few examples of confidence-related challenges that negotiators encounter.

- Being afraid to ask for what they want
- Conflict aversion
- Fear of asserting their position and saying 'no'
- Feeling uncomfortable with winning

Confidence is a challenge regardless of whether you do not have enough, or you have too much of it. However, in most cases, difficulties occur when you don't have enough confidence. For instance, you might be asking yourself: 'Am I a good negotiator?' 'Do I have what it takes to win?' 'Am I strong enough?' 'Will I succeed?' These questions showcase self-doubt, and it is something that the other party will spot and might use to their own advantage.

Some negotiators do not have the courage to say 'no'. Rejecting a proposal does not necessarily mean the end of the negotiation. On the contrary, it could mean that your negotiation partner might see you as someone who has better options and is ready to stand their ground, or even leave the discussion. This might cause them to reconsider their position. Remember that you negotiate to attain your goals. You should not enter an agreement that will leave you worse off. Do not be afraid that refusing will hinder your relationship with your counterparty. If it does, then it means the partnership would not last anyway, because it was one-sided.

On the other hand, an individual can be overly confident. That person might believe that they are in the best position, which will lead them to impose their own ideas and solutions. If you identify with these issues, there are simple things that you can do to overcome this challenge. Remind yourself that negotiation is a discussion. For a discussion to have a satisfactory outcome, there should be mutual communication and understanding. You should give the time to your counterparty to think, to consider before they answer your questions and to speak their thoughts. If you come across as overly confident, you will shut your negotiation partner off, who in return might become defensive and not willing to cooperate.

How to overcome confidence-related challenges: VCR technique

If you read my book, *Negotiate Your Way to Success,* you will be familiar with the visualisation–confidence–realisation (VCR) method. Visualisation is the creation of anticipatory emotions. It involves setting a goal, imagining what success will feel like and directing the efforts towards the desired outcome according to a negotiation plan. Confidence relates to being internally convinced that we deserve what we are asking for and clearly communicating our demands. Realisation is putting the plan into action with purpose and conviction.

For example, if you negotiate a salary increase the visualisation part will relate to imagining what you will be able to do with the additional income and how liberating it will be not to have to worry about financial constraints. This is a strong motivator towards the achievement of your predetermined goal (salary increase). Confidence comes from being aware of all the efforts we have put into getting that raise. Many people underestimate their own worth or the value of what they do. Realisation means asking for what we deserve with conviction. The VCR technique will help you step into the negotiation with a positive and confident mindset.

Strategic challenges

The following are a few examples of strategic-oriented challenges that negotiators encounter.

- Putting all the cards on the table, creating too much momentum at the beginning, then not having anything else to offer during the rest of the process.
- Jumping into the process before agreeing on the rules.
- Moving too quickly for the close.
- Rushing to find a speedy compromise.

While challenges related to emotions management or levels of confidence are strictly intrinsic, strategic challenges are both intrinsic and extrinsic. Those who are governed by feelings rather than reason often enter the negotiation on the spur of the moment, without proper preparation; or their strategic execution crumbles in the heat of the negotiations. Lack of confidence can also adversely impact the strategic implementation. If you enter a negotiation with fear, hesitation and no conviction, you can have the best strategy, but you will not win to the full potential.

These challenges might exist before the discussions start or they might surface during the negotiation when you feel that you are not negotiating from a position of power. For example, it might become frustrating when you realise that your negotiation partner is not taking you seriously. This is often the concern expressed by junior or female negotiators. In this case, you should not allow your frustration to get the best of you and should politely stand your ground. There is no need to battle out who is in a power position. This will take focus away from the objective you want to achieve. Focus on the prize, not on personal attacks. You should show why you deserve a place at the table by being in control of your agenda and by strategic execution.

A common mistake is that the negotiator wants to speed up the deal-making. The best outcomes in high-stakes negotiations hardly ever emerge from a rushed negotiation process. It takes time to build trust to reach a mutual agreement, a critical condition for partnerships. Most importantly, time works to *your* advantage. It allows you to calm your emotions, to work up the confidence you need and to unfold your strategy. Patience is key.

Furthermore, you should not view a negotiation as a one-time process. In many cases you negotiate to close a deal, but also to build a long-term relationship. By quickly looking to close, you might miss certain opportunities you were not aware of. The best example is the negotiator who puts all the cards on the table at the beginning or commits too early at the start. By doing so, they will have limited bargaining power left, which will leave them destabilised and insecure.

This book is designed to address the most common challenges. On one hand, it serves as a strategic guide through the negotiation process; on the other, it equips you with practical tips and psychological tools for self-empowerment.

How to overcome strategic challenges: Negotiation pre-mortem technique

Usually we know exactly what could have been done better once the deal falls through. Imagining what you could lose is the best preventive measure from it actually happening. A pre-mortem is a fictional scenario in which you anticipate that your negotiation has already failed. It will help you identify deficiencies in your strategy that your negotiation partner might detect and use against you.

How does this work? When you prepare for a negotiation, draft up a negotiation plan along with the best-case scenario. Then write yourself a rejection letter. Put yourself in the shoes of the other party and make it as real as possible. If you are having trouble writing the rejection yourself, ask a trusted advisor to draft and send it to you.

Negotiation pre-mortem example

Dear Negotiator,

Thank you for entrusting us with your business proposal. The procurement department at our firm has now considered all the proposals they received. Despite your interesting offering, I regret to inform you that they have decided not to give your proposal the green light. State the reasons here . . .

We greatly appreciate your interest in cooperating with us and wish you every success for your future business.

Yours sincerely,

Expert view

Dr Robert Cialdini
Author, keynote speaker and president of Influence at Work, USA

Pre-suasion can be used to empower ourselves to achieve certain goals. I remember when I was in graduate school getting my PhD. There were six of us in the doctorate program. One of my colleagues continuously achieved 99 per cent in his exams. We always wondered how he managed to get such high scores. After all, he wasn't any smarter than us. When I asked him how he did it, he drew my attention to an interesting phenomenon.

When you stand outside the doors of the exam room, you encounter many other students. Usually they are worried and stressed about the upcoming test. The majority focus on the weaknesses and shortcomings that might make them fail. This mood is contagious. If you succumb to it, it will eventually have a debilitating effect on you. His approach was different. He would focus on his past successes that he achieved by hard work. While others stood there demotivated, he couldn't wait to start.

▶

People who have a concern that they will not do well will quit when faced with a roadblock. Those who have confidence that they can do well will persist in the face of adversity. My advice is to give yourself a sense of capacity that encourages persistence and motivates you to push further. Spend time on remembering your previous successes to instil a sense of confidence in yourself. Don't focus on deficiencies. Thinking about past victories produces subsequent positive outcomes. Power posing does not do the trick. The secret lies in your mind. Fill your mind with achievement-related memories to empower yourself.

Aside from overcoming challenges, it is recommended that you reinforce positive habits and cultivate principles of ethical conduct. In the end, you become what you do. Based on my practice, I have compiled a list of desirable traits and behaviours. Here are the ten commandments of a classy and efficient negotiator.

The Negotiator's Commandments

1 Be clear about intentions.
2 Be respectful.
3 Have an open mind.
4 Be flexible and open to negotiate.
5 Be accountable.
6 Be likeable.
7 Be communicative.
8 Act with integrity.
9 Know your boundaries and never compromise your values.
10 Do no harm.

Summary of key take-aways

1 The most important negotiator you have to win over is you.
2 A negotiation is a human-to-human interaction.

3   Negotiation challenges are universal; chances are you and the other negotiator shares the same ones.

4   You have control over your psyche and only you can claim your negotiation power.

5   Focus on your strengths, and do not allow your challenges to hold you back.

The article 'Negotiation is tough and should be left to professionals' by Andrew Hill explores some of the reasons why negotiations are often seen as difficult.

Negotiation is tough and should be left to professionals

By Andrew Hill

Financial Times, 20 January 2020

'This is harder than real estate in New York, Jared, isn't it?' Donald Trump joked to his son-in-law Jared Kushner during a lengthy preamble to last week's White House signing of a 'phase one' trade deal with China. Framed as a humble-brag from one property tycoon to another, Mr Trump's rhetorical question inadvertently exposed a truth: most negotiation is tough, complex work that resists simple formulas such as those the US president laid out in his 1987 bestseller *Trump: The Art of the Deal*. There, he summarised his approach this way: 'I aim very high, and then I just keep pushing and pushing to get what I'm after.' This is not the place to analyse the US-China deal in detail, but it is hard to agree with Mr Trump's description of this preliminary truce in the trade war as 'an incredible breakthrough'. That both sides remain at odds over many of the issues that triggered the hostilities does not bode well for a rapid conclusion to phase two. Experienced negotiators on both sides will hope their bosses stay out of those talks. 'Everyone thinks they're a negotiator and they think they should be wheeled in to save the day', according to a friend who has spent the past three decades parleying with governments and companies on behalf of a large multinational. 'But the more senior the person that does the deal, the worse the deal.' He describes his role as 'creating order out of the chaos' of scraps of paper and heads of agreement signed by his superiors. The start and the end of the process is bound to involve the sort of flummery staged in Washington DC last week, or the previous week's sparring between Boris Johnson and new European Commission president Ursula von der Leyen ahead of forthcoming Brexit talks. When it comes to haggling over the detail, though, that should be left to gimlet-eyed

➡

professionals with experience, humility and boundless patience. Viewing negotiations as a competition rather than as a trade-off and relying on persuasion to win the day are just two of the reasons most deals disappoint. Negotiation consultancy Scotwork has just surveyed nearly 5,000 untrained negotiators in 31 countries about their experience doing business deals. Less than a quarter of their negotiations ended in stronger relationships and higher long-term value. Among other weaknesses, inexperienced dealmakers admitted to a lack of preparation and ethical lapses. For instance, 38 per cent of sellers said they thought it was acceptable to lie to their counterparts.

What Mr Trump might paint as a strength – 'I just keep pushing' – can be a fatal weakness. Not enough people go into negotiations thinking 'what can I concede?', says Scotwork director Richard Savage. 'If [they] don't recognise that this is a trading process, a portcullis drops down and behaviour starts to go downhill.' In skilfully handled business deals, the negotiation is both more subtle and more collaborative. For instance, clever dealmakers will ensure they have a number of 'pigeons' ready to offer to their counterparty. These are items of limited value that can be made to sound like important concessions, to be given up in exchange for a genuinely valuable counter-offer. If they spot a worthless pigeon coming their way, they should indignantly expose it as a 'Barmecide', named after the rich man in the Arabian Nights, who served an imaginary feast to a beggar. In the Brexit negotiations, it seemed as though such subtlety was lacking. Professional negotiators were dismayed by the UK's reckless use of 'red lines', beyond which it claimed it could not step, and its setting of deadlines that sounded firm but turned out to be fungible. It was no surprise to Mr Savage that initial negotiations foundered after the 2016 referendum. 'The ultimate cause was arrogance and intransigence', he says. Mr Johnson's change of style at least unblocked the process, but, looking forward, my negotiator friend worries about 'the sheer complexity of the things that need to be negotiated and about the ridiculousness of the timescale: I know how long it takes to negotiate with one party, let alone 27 [EU members]'. Training provider Scotwork concludes, a little self-servingly, that negotiators need training. Such skills are 'as applicable in family disputes, house-buying and child-raising as when you're a gold-miner negotiating with an Ashanti king', says Mr Savage. The more important lesson, though, is that most buyers will continue to have to deal with their suppliers long after the contract is squared away, just as the US will have to go on trading with China, even after phase two, and the UK with the EU after Brexit. Few relationships end with the signing ceremony, so it makes sense not to leave either side nursing a lingering resentment about what happened during the horse-trading.

 Source: Hill, A. Negotiation is tough and should be left to professionals. *Financial Times*, January 20, 2020.

Further reading

1   Burg, B. and Mann, J.D. (2018) *The Go-Giver Influencer. A Little Story About a Most Persuasive Idea.* New York: Portfolio/Penguin.

2   Carnegie, D. (2006) *How to Win Friends and Influence People.* London: Vermilion.

3   Cialdini, R. (2021) *Influence. The Psychology of Persuasion.* New York: Harper Collins Publishers.

4   Cialdini, R. (2016) *Pre-Suasion. A Revolutionary Way to Influence and Persuade.* London: Random House Books.

5   Cuddy, A. (2016) *Presence. Bringing Your Boldest Self to Your Biggest Challenges.* London: Orion.

6   Ellenberger, H.F. (1970) *The Discovery of the Unconscious. The History and Evolution of Dynamic Psychiatry.* New York: Basic Books Inc. Publishers.

7   Greene, R. (1998) *The 48 Laws of Power.* London: Profile Books Ltd.

8   Jagodzinska, K. (2020) *Negotiation Booster. The Ultimate Self-Empowerment Guide to High-Impact Negotiations.* New York: Business Expert Press.

9   Jagodzinska, K. (2021) *Negotiate Your Way to Success: Personal Guidelines to Boost Your Career.* New York: Business Expert Press.

CHAPTER 2
DEFINING THE NEGOTIATION MISSION STATEMENT

'Would you tell me, please, which way I ought to go from here?' – asked Alice.

'That depends a good deal on where you want to get to', said the Cat.

'I don't much care where', said Alice.

'Then it doesn't matter which way you go', said the Cat.

Lewis Carroll, Alice in Wonderland

What you will discover in this chapter:

- How to write the negotiation mission statement, and make it work in practice
- Practical tips for designing the mission statement
- Negotiation mission cheat sheet

What is negotiation?

In order to define the negotiation mission and value statement it would be beneficial to have a closer look at what a negotiation is. Why do we negotiate? The classic definition assumes the existence of two parties with different and common (otherwise there would be no negotiation) needs who are trying to reach a mutually acceptable agreement. The discussion usually involves the distribution of a limited resource, or the perception of a limitation placed on a desired resource. This sounds familiar to anyone who has ever read any book on the topic of negotiation. Consequently, business practitioners have learned to operate within the boundaries set forth by this conceptualisation. The word 'boundaries' was used deliberately, because negotiation is often approached as a means to a narrow end – closing a deal. In reality, the scope of a negotiation is much broader than the deal itself.

Negotiation is a whole eco-system. It unfolds on three levels, as shown in Figure 2.1. The central point is always the individual – each party with their needs, interests, hopes, fears, pre-occupations and expectations. Consequently, negotiation begins with self-management of the internal factors that drive the outward negotiation behaviour. Then there is the internal level – the negotiations which involve the members of the same negotiation team who discuss the terms of a deal among themselves. The last level is the external interaction between two negotiators from opposite sides. This is the moment when the representatives of both parties engage in an exchange directed at finding an outcome that satisfies or satisfices (satisfies to a minimum). The classic definition of a negotiation embraces only the last level. The risk of a singularly external-oriented focus might lead to the lack of understanding of the internal processes and practices that influence the effectiveness of the organisation as a whole.

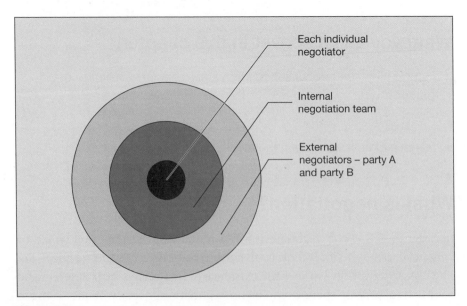

Figure 2.1 Negotiation eco-system

Negotiation is not only a tool for deal-making. It is one of the core operational activities. No matter the industry, the part of the world and regardless of the line of business, a lot of company time is spent on negotiating. Business professionals often tell me that they negotiate from dawn to dusk, each single day. These are huge costs (both sunk and opportunity) in terms of allocation of resources and time investment. It is surprising that so few organisations attribute a concrete monetary value to the negotiation process; they do only to its end product – the deal.

Agent Gary Noesner, the former Chief of the Crisis Negotiation Unit at the FBI, took part in many life and death negotiations, including the controversial Waco siege.[1] Negotiations with hostage takers are indisputably the highest-stakes negotiations. Agent Noesner recalls that after a mission was completed, the FBI officials were often curious to know what made the hostage taker surrender. The answer usually was: 'We do not recall exactly what you said that made us come out, but we liked the way it made us feel'. Could this be a recipe for operational success? Have you ever asked your client or business partner why they chose to close the deal with you and not your competitor? Chances are that the responses would be similar to those expressed by the hostage takers.

A negotiation is not the means of closing a deal, but rather the engine for reaching (and successfully executing) your overall organisational mission. Therefore, the negotiation mission itself should be clearly defined. A mission will create a distinctive negotiation culture – an approach that all your negotiators follow, and which will differentiate you from all the other negotiators. Whereas almost every company has a mission and value statement, few (if any) set forth a specific negotiation mission. This is a serious omission in relation to one of the core drivers of organisational effectiveness and success.

What is a negotiation mission statement?

Most resources suggest that a negotiation should start with setting the goal and objective (these two topics will be addressed in more detail in Chapters 3 and 4). This sequence might work if negotiations were performed in a vacuum.

---

[1] The Waco siege was a 51-day standoff between the cult members of Branch Davidians and FBI agents. It ended on 19 April 1993, when the religious group's compound near Waco, Texas, was destroyed in a fire. As a result, nearly 80 people were killed, including federal agents, pregnant women, children and other cult members, among them the cult leader, David Koresh.

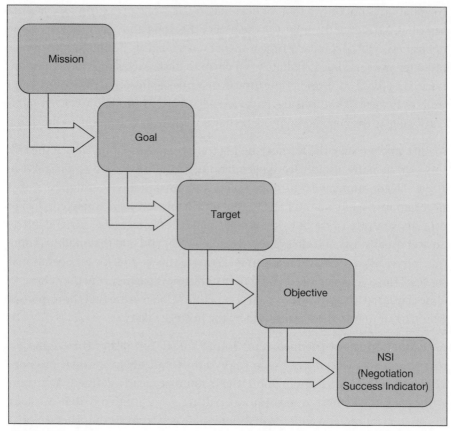

Figure 2.2 The process from mission to negotiation success

In reality, a negotiation is seldom isolated from the overall context of operational activities. A negotiation mission is much broader than the objective and the target. It is the starting point for the whole negotiation process from mission to negotiation success attainment, as illustrated by Figure 2.2.

If there is no mission, all the individual negotiators will apply their habitual negotiation approach. They will engage in creative negotiating, with each actor operating according to their individual preferences, rules and standards. The result will be a mosaic of negotiation styles and a lack of a distinctive flavour that the other business partners can recognise and appreciate.

Negotiations aside, think for a moment about what happens to the companies with no overarching operational mission. How can the employees know which direction to go, and how can the customers and other stakeholders know what to expect from doing business with the company? Even though the omission of a mission is obviously counterproductive when viewed from a company perspective, this is exactly what is lacking in the negotiation arena.

The purpose of a mission is to announce exactly where you are heading, both internally and externally. Values depict those behaviours and actions that will help get you there. They need to be concrete and not leave too much margin for interpretation. Having a clear sense of direction and knowing what to do to get there has many advantages. Perhaps the key advantage of a mission is that it allows focus and a directional effort. Energy and time can be channelled into goal achievement instead of questioning each step. Furthermore, a mission statement attributes meaning to the activity. According to C. G. Jung (*Collected Works 7*, p. 224) to achieve meaning requires the deepest possible understanding of a situation and the bringing together of what were previously experienced as separate elements within a situation. In other words, we can achieve meaning when we recognise certain patterns.

In order to define a mission statement, it is helpful to start with the fundamental question: *How will we win?* This question will serve as a screening mechanism. It will require you to make choices about the allocation of time and other precious resources. As a result, those discussions, meetings, calls and other components of the negotiation process that will prevent you from winning a high-stakes negotiation will be limited. Each decision, such as making a concession or placing a demand, will then be linked to the mission statement.

The *'How will we win?'* question has a dual nature. It is task-oriented in the sense that it is focused on winning, understood as the maximisation of monetary gains. On the other hand, it is values-oriented: it forces you to choose which behaviours you will accept (and which not) in order to achieve your win. As you will discover later based on the examples of company mission statements, an effective mission statement usually balances two aspects: the tangible and the intangible.

The template in the following figure can be used to help you establish your negotiation mission. You will notice that it incorporates certain values that support the mission.

Negotiation mission cheat sheet

- Take a look at your company mission statement to identify your core organisational values.

- Are any of these values already reflected in your negotiation approach? If so, which ones? Which ones are missing?

- How do you want your company to come across in negotiations – as competitive, cooperative, future-oriented, customer-focused?

- Incorporate those values in your negotiation mission statement.

- Align the mission with clear objectives and principles.

- Make sure the mission is operational.

Negotiation mission cheat sheet – Practical application example

- Let's assume that the mission of your organisation is to primarily serve your customers.

- If this is the case, your ideal long-term outcome of the negotiation will be a sustainable and long-lasting agreement.

- Now consider how you will communicate that mindset to the other party.

- To reflect this customer-centred approach in your negotiation mission statement, you could incorporate the following values: collaboration, win-win mindset, client for life mentality, succeeding together, partnership.

- Align the mission with clear objectives, such as relationship versus task-orientation only, transparency, profitability understood as a sum of financial gain and relationship strengthening.

- Make the mission statement operational. You should introduce monitoring procedures to make sure that the external negotiators 'walk-the-talk' in their dealings with clients.

- Eliminate any deviations from the mission and supporting values before they become a new, undesired mission.

Negotiation mission example:

The mission of our company is to procure value-adding services for our clients through mutual engagement in the quest for sustainable business relations.

A company mission statement is typically set up by top management. By analogy, a negotiation mission statement should be defined by the person highest in hierarchy, the decision maker (and not the negotiator who is the executive force). A negotiation culture flows from the top, first internally and then it is manifested externally.

The secret of a successful implementation lies in the values – the means to an end of the mission. Therefore, it seems logical that the negotiation mission and values need to be mutually reinforcing. The reason why many negotiations fail is due to a disconnect between the mission (or the complete lack thereof) and the values. When I conduct in-house negotiation trainings, I often see mission statements on huge posters displayed in the corridors of the company head-quarters. They serve as a constant reminder of what the company stands for and where it strives to be. When I introduce the idea of weaving in the company mission statement and values as a fundament for the negotiation, the sugges-tion is usually met with vivid interest combined with surprise as to why this has not been thought of earlier.

Key points to take into account when preparing a negotiation mission statement:

- Agreeing on common values that will support the negotiation mission is a critical success factor. The implication of this is the need for management and negotia-tors to identify unique and common characteristics of an organisation and to express these in their negotiation mission and value statements.

- Companies which build their mission statements around the implementation of various resources and relationships seem to be more capable of improved perfor-mance. A narrow focus on growth alone does not seem to enhance performance.

- The individual perceptions of the representatives of organisations will impact the defining of the mission statement. It is therefore essential to understand the perception of the mission of the organisation from the perspective of the people who will be communicating the mission on behalf of the company and then implementing it in the negotiation process.

Only advocates of the mission can come across as genuine negotiators. This consideration should be addressed before the negotiation mission statement is defined. Alignment between the negotiators' perception and the intended negotia-tion mission is a critical condition for implementation of the mission.

When establishing a mission, the personal values of each negotiator need to be considered, because they will serve as the start point and later on as a guide to ethical deal-making behaviours. Therefore, negotiators should be designated in accordance to the personal values that they represent: balancing individual values in a negotiation with the interests of the organisation (the agent-principal dilemma).

One of the toughest ethical problems for managers and negotiators is the potential for the existence of conflicts of interest, which requires them to balance the values of their organisation with their own needs. Negotiating on behalf of yourself might be easier in this matter, since you are more likely to reject the possibility of a personal advantage in order to preserve your sense of integrity. However, when you negotiate as a representative of the company, the burden of your integrity may seem less heavy. An individual negotiator is always at more risk in terms of ethics in a collective setting, since they are stripped of individual responsibility.

Conflict resolution mechanisms need to be in place in the event that a conflict over deeply held values occurs. Should this be the case, the decisive factor should be whether the values serve the overall efficiency of the negotiation process. It might sometimes be necessary to make concessions on a core value to induce overall cooperation, provided that the fundamental value system does not collapse. It is helpful to evaluate which values are truly sacred. Since value conflicts often arise when parties consider their values to be non-negotiable, it is important to determine whether they are objectively non-negotiable or pseudo-sacred (non-negotiable under certain conditions and negotiable when the conditions change). For example, negotiators with weak alternatives are more likely to compromise on sacred values or issues.

Organisations look up to their leaders to establish the vision and values. Therefore, leaders should take into consideration the various single values and interests to then establish holistic norms for the organisation as a whole. This approach will allow them to negotiate buy-in and support from their followers.

The negotiation mission is perceived as the engine for the operational implementation of the core objectives and values that drive the negotiation. Therefore, a clearly defined mission is the prerequisite to operational implementation of the principles. In an ideal scenario, there should be a bridge between profitability and other, not-quantifiable elements. Insights shared by business leaders suggest that there is a need to formalise the 'what we want to get' – this relates to addressing the *'How will we win?'* question and including the answer to it in the long-term strategic negotiation plan.

Expert view

René Koets
Partner and Head of Management Consulting at KPMG, Switzerland

The negotiation mission in high-stakes deals is more related to objectives and principles than a concrete mission; it is more operational. The key principle that drives my negotiation behaviour is that I only believe in outcome deals when there is a win–win. In high-stakes negotiations we have to be prepared to walk away if a win–win is not possible. In order for a win–win outcome to be possible, there need to be clear objectives understood as a certain profitability, as well as a probability of success of the project we sell, which for me means that I can deliver what I promised. Transparency is important: both sides need to know what they are getting into in order to get a deal that is beneficial for both. The challenge may be that certain objectives are formalised, such as the quantifiable factors, while others are not, such as the evaluation of deals in the long term. The sum of both these factors, the overall 'what we want to get' is not always formalised enough.

I do not believe in 'buying deals'. What this means is, for example, to offer a project cheaper just for the sake of winning, and later on trying to recuperate the losses by upselling. This will eventually backfire, in the form of a broken relationship with the other side. I prefer a 'client for life' approach. We want to be able to look each other in the eye. Initial dropping of profitability or project price reduction is possible in cases when we want to get into a certain market. However, the reasons for this need to be made clear in order not to create a pattern of certain financial expectations from the other side and leave them feeling surprised if the profitability increases later on.

We have a set-up in which the partners are responsible for not only getting the deal, but also delivering the deal. This means working with the other party in the long run. They need to be conscious of the consequences of their actions and take responsibility for the task and client relationship.

The underlying values for negotiating high-stakes deals are: clear objectives, transparency, striving for longevity ('Client for life' mindset) and being aware of the future consequences of the deal.

An analysis of company mission and value statements of the world's top companies can serve as an inspiration for setting forth of a negotiation mission. I invite you to go and take a look at their websites.

How you can apply this in your negotiation mission: Be crystal clear about what you want to achieve. Ensure that the mission and values work together as a winning proposition.

Use the formula: W–H–M (What–How–Means): What do you want to do, how you intend to do it and by which means. Then season it with supporting values.

One could argue that most companies actually have negotiation mission and value statements that exist on the internal level, even though these are not publicly displayed. Sharing this information with the broader public could be seen as a disadvantage for them, since it would be easier for the counterpart to analyse and adapt their own strategy. Based on my exchanges with executives involved in negotiating deals across the globe, this is not the case. Defining the negotiation mission and value statement is not a common practice, on the internal or external level.

Your turn to practice

Our negotiation mission is to . . . . (*insert what you want to achieve*) by . . . . (*specify by which means*) in order to . . . . (*input your ultimate objective*).

Our core values:

– *List 3–4 supporting values that connect the mission to concrete principles*

– *Some examples: transparency, integrity, collaboration, creativity*

Summary of key take-aways

1 Omission of a clearly defined negotiation mission is a strategic disadvantage.

2 The purpose of a mission is to announce exactly where you are heading, both internally and externally in the high-stakes negotiation.

3 Values depict those behaviours and actions that will help get you there.

4 Start by answering the question: *How will we win?*

5 Ensure that the mission and values support each other.

Further reading

1 Dermol, V. (2013) *Relationship between Mission Statement and Company Performance*. International School for Social and Business Studies Celje, Slovenia, January 2013.

2 Jung, C.G. (1953) *Two Essays on Analytical Psychology. Collected Works*. Vol. 7. New York: Pantheon Books.

3 Khalifa, A.S. (2012) *Mission, Purpose, and Ambition: Redefining the Mission Statement*. University of Sharjah, United Arab Emirates, 03.08.2012.

4 Mowles, C. (2008) *Values in International Development of Organisations: Negotiating Non-Negotiables*. 21 Jan 2008.

5 Spear, S. (2017) *Impression Management Activity in Vision, Mission, and Values Statements: A Comparison of Commercial and Charitable Organizations*. University of the West of England, Bristol, UK, 3.03.2017.

6 Welch, J. and Welch, S. (2005) *Winning*. HarperCollins.

7 Williams S. (2019) *The Financial Times Guides, Business Start Up, 2019/20 edition. The Most Comprehensive Guide for Entrepreneurs*. FT Publishing. (See: Chapter 11: Names and brands)

CHAPTER 3
SETTING THE GOAL

'Leadership is working with goals and vision; management is working with objectives.'

Russel L. Honoré

What you will discover in this chapter:

- Why it is important to have a clear goal
- How to set goals in a high-stakes negotiation and link them with targets
- What are the challenges and pitfalls that can undermine the effectiveness of goals

Beware of what can happen if you do not have a clear goal

You already know that the mission statement provides a focused direction for the negotiation. It indicates the values and behaviours that will lead you or your firm to a successful negotiation outcome. A goal is a concrete plan to be achieved to fulfil the mission. It is what drives the negotiation process towards the desired end state, such as signing a deal, entering a partnership or agreeing on a set of terms for a given transaction. Setting a goal is one of the first things that needs to be done before a negotiation starts. Improvisation is great; however, entering a negotiation without a clear goal is a risky move. One CEO learned this lesson the hard way.

It was a late Friday afternoon in Paris and the CEO of one of the big international firms was just about to leave his office. He was more than ready for a relaxing weekend that would start with a nice dinner in one of his favourite bistros: the type that tourists have never heard about. It had been a long week, several strenuous weeks actually. The year end was the time when all the strategic decisions were being taken. Top management of the company were busy with goal setting that would steer the company towards success or leave it behind its competitors. The flow of meetings and demands on their time seemed never ending. Apart from the usual year end frenzy, the company was going through an important transition that involved shifts in the organisational chart. The implementation of this process relied heavily on the support of the HR department.

As the CEO was closing up the last files on his computer, the chief of the HR department popped her head in his office door. 'Do you have a minute', she asked, 'I need to ask you something quickly'. Quickly was the magic word that made him comply with her request. He could handle quickly, just hear her out and be off to wine and dine. He stood up immediately and followed her to the meeting room. True to her word, she did not waste much time with getting to the point.

What the chief of the HR wanted turned out to be a huge demand that involved a significant salary increase, among other smaller requests. Should she not get what she was asking for, she would hand in her resignation notice on Monday. The request was tricky. The firm had just introduced a salary increase freeze to cope with the financial difficulties it had been facing. There would be no bonuses nor any other financial rewards this year. Due to internal restructuring and cost saving policies, regular employees were being let go.

The CEO felt like someone pulled the rug from underneath his feet. His first thought was that they had been working together for the past seven years and he was not ready to lose her. In addition, her role was pivotal in the ongoing transition. If she left before the process was completed, the success of the whole undertaking would be at a risk; this would have severe consequences for the future of the company. A high-stakes negotiation was certainly not what he was expecting nor prepared for on a late Friday afternoon. Without a second thought he agreed with her demands. He then went out for his dinner. Somehow the food did not taste the same that evening. Nor did the wine.

Negotiation consists of three driving forces: the individual governed by their motives and a multitude of emotions, the task that needs to be achieved (making a deal) and the relationship between the parties (the partnership). A properly defined goal will allow for a purposeful discussion that embraces all these three factors.

On the individual level, once you know what your goal is, you can adapt the appropriate behaviours and responses that will help you achieve it. This means that you will most likely be driven by reason rather than emotions, at least in the long run. The CEO shared his story with me during our coaching. We had 20 sessions together. Nineteen of them involved going back to the situation with the chief of the HR. We analysed it from every possible angle, to the point that we started referring to our work as negotiation-psychoanalysis. Even after considerable time had passed, he still had strong feelings about the whole event. I suspect that had he known that the discussion would turn into a high-stakes negotiation, he would not have gone in without first establishing his own goal.

While the link between goal setting and the individual level may be more elusive, the goal in relation to the task execution is clearly visible. In terms of the task realisation, setting the goal will serve as a checkpoint. A helpful question may be: *'Am I on track to reaching my goal?'*. Negotiators are often reminded to keep their eye on the prize. Even the mind's eye cannot cope if one does not know what the goal actually is. The CEO did not have a precise idea about what the goal of the negotiation was – whether it was to safeguard the firm's interests in a rough time, or to preserve the relationship with his chief of HR, or perhaps to save his own face when she confronted him with the tough demands.

Depending on what the goal is, the focus of the negotiation can switch from pure task-orientation to more relational. If the goal of a high-stakes negotiation is to build a long-lasting partnership, for example in a joint venture negotiation or in the case of companies that have a 'client for life' approach, then the relationship aspect will be the guiding light for the end goal. The reason for the CEO's dilemma might have been a disconnect between the parties' goals. Once he learned that the 'quick ask' was in fact a tough negotiation, the CEO's first thought was that he does not want to lose his chief of HR, not at that moment and not after all these years spent working together. Perhaps her approach was strictly task-driven. Or maybe it was her strategy to take him by surprise.

The three-step guide to setting goals

1 Understand what motivates you

The different ways of approaching the goal-setting process will be reflected in the negotiation outcome. How negotiators approach goal setting has an impact on what they can achieve, both on the internal (self-empowerment) level and from a strategic perspective. It should be noted that the same desired end does not necessarily call for the same approach. Preferences will vary from one negotiator to another: there is no one-size-fits-all solution. Goal setting and attainment are closely linked to motivation. Understanding what motivates an individual is the prerequisite to establishing a goal that they can strive to reach. A properly defined goal has to tick two boxes. From the strategic standpoint, it needs to be aligned with the desired negotiation outcome. On the self-empowerment level, it has to stimulate the negotiator. Many negotiations fail because the goals are strategically set without taking into consideration the negotiator, their profile, preferences, habits and tendencies. The negotiator is seen as the tool for goal execution. The executives with whom I work often confide in me that they do not believe in the goals that have been passed down to them, usually by the people higher in the hierarchy. In a top-down approach to goal setting, the negotiator lacks a sense of ownership, which is a critical factor for goal achievement.

2 Choose the right approach

Goal setting can be performed using the promotion or prevention approach. A promotion focus tends to view goals as a hope, wish or aspiration and is pursued by focusing on the positive outcome. A prevention focus sees the goal as a duty, responsibility or obligation which in contrast is pursued by preventing negative outcomes. Promotion-focused negotiators are more likely to reach optimal integrative solutions, because they care most about reaching their ideal goal. With that in mind they are motivated to consider flexible ways of achieving their goals. This is hardly surprising. A focus on positive outcomes will create anticipatory emotions linked to future states. Anticipatory emotions are feelings that can be invoked by imagining how it would feel to have already reached a certain status. Happiness is addictive and the power of the mind is limitless in its creativity to achieve and maintain it. If it can be imagined, it can be done.

3 Aim like a winner

There is plenty of research that supports the benefits of aiming high in relation to the task aspect. What I often hear in pre-negotiation meetings is, '*At a minimum we must achieve . . .* '. Once this phrase is used, it is fairly easy to predict that the minimum will in fact be what is achieved in the negotiation itself. A skilled negotiator at the other side of the table will notice the moment they hit your minimum goal. Subtle telltales such as relaxing of the body and less energy invested in the further pursuit of the goal are clues as to what your goal threshold is.

Here are the positives of aiming high.

- Setting specific as well as challenging goals (such as, for example, negotiating a 20 per cent higher rate than on past projects) can lead to better objective outcomes than setting vague and lower goals.

- Highly ambitious negotiators contribute to more efficient agreements for all parties involved.

- Aspirational goals invite creativity and innovation in finding new ways to achieve them.

- Aiming high by setting challenging goals motivates negotiators to work harder and to stretch the negotiation limits.

- Once a higher goal is achieved, it opens the doors for future ambitious goals to be reached. Setting higher goals can create a culture and habit of success.

While aiming high is the recommended approach, there may be a backlash effect. First, setting goals that consistently cannot be reached can have a demotivating effect on future performance. The threshold between high and unattainable goals needs to be carefully considered.

Second, ambitious goals seem to work so well that the counterpart may resent the negotiators' success. Consequently, the negotiator is perceived as unlikable and the relationship can be damaged. This is not necessarily relevant for one-off negotiations, but considering future interactions, it is important to find the balance between the desire to meet a high goal as well as the need to build a good relationship.

A strategic guide to setting goals

- Goals should be formulated in a clear and precise way. Abstraction should be avoided. The more specific a goal is, the easier it will be for you (and your negotiator partner) to know what exactly you want to obtain, and to adopt behaviours directed towards achieving the goal.

▶

For example, *We need to stop losing accounts* is an imprecisely stated goal. It would be better to state: *We need to win at least nine new accounts by the end of Q1 202X.*

- A goal should be measurable. The negotiation process should be chopped into phases, and progress towards goal achievement should be monitored according to pre-defined key goal indicators (KGI).

  Using the example *We need to win at least nine new accounts by the end of Q1 202X,* progress can be measured in each month of Q1. If we manage to obtain three new accounts by the end of January, then we know we are on the right track in the first month of the quarter.

- The goals should be challenging and continuously improved over time through monitoring and review of what worked and what didn't.

- It is helpful to use the following formula adopted from the singer Cher: *If I could turn back time.* After each negotiation, ask yourself how you would set the goal if you could turn back the hands of time in the negotiation and do it all over again. Would there be anything you would change in relation to the goal definition and execution?

- Ambitious goals can be overwhelming. In order to stay motivated, it is helpful to break down larger goals into more digestible, smaller ones. A tiny step after step is better than complete standstill.

  Using the example *We need to win at least nine new accounts by the end of Q1 202X,* the goal can be made easier by breaking it down into smaller action items: *We need to make ten new client calls each day to win nine new accounts.*

- Fairness should be used with caution. Reaching a 'fair' agreement is not a goal, because there is no such thing as splitting the pie fairly. Fairness is not a neutral metric. What is fair to one party may greatly differ from the perception of what is fair according to the other.

- A goal should bridge the task (T) and the relationship (R). The nature of the deal will therefore shape the goal setting. For long-term partnerships, the focus will be a balance between the T and R elements. For one-off transactions, the goal may be based on the task only.

- A goal should be formulated in a positive, future- and action-oriented manner. Be proactive in setting the goal, otherwise you will end up in the passenger seat, being driven in the direction of the goal of your negotiation partner.

- It is helpful to use the failure-proof formula: *By x I will have achieved y.* For example, 'Sales will increase by 10 per cent in the next quarter'. Or 'By 31 January, we will sign the deal/enter into a partnership with company ABC'.

- A properly defined goal should indicate the three Ws – Who, What and When. Who is responsible for achieving what and by when is the result expected?

What is the correlation between goal and target setting?

After the goal is set, targets help assess the desired outcome in measurable and specific terms. While some sources use the terms 'goals' and 'targets' interchangeably, targets are often expressed in monetary terms, for example a percentage decrease or increase.

Managerial theory calls for defining SMARTER targets and goals. This popular acronym stands for Specific, Measurable, Attainable, Relevant, Time-bound, Ethical and Rewarding. A target should be specific, which will allow the negotiator to know exactly what they are aiming for. It is like typing an end destination into a GPS system. A specific address is not only the country, but also the city, the street and the number. A measurable target sets benchmarks for assessing achievement. For example, the successful completion of a given project can be measured by a percentage change of number of closed deals or client accounts landed. Attainable goals stretch the limits, but nonetheless remain within the realm of what is possible to achieve in a given situation, with a specific business partner, using the available resources and while operating in a specific economic, ethical and legal context. Realistic goals use past performance assessment as a predictor of future results under the current conditions of the negotiation. Relevance relates to how the goal aligns with values and what is its importance in relation to the negotiation mission. Time-bound calls for placing a time limit for the achievement of the goal. A high-stakes negotiation involves significant investment of time, one of the most precious resources. Managing the time lapse and measuring the time spent against the return on the investment are the best ways of monitoring what makes sense and how much time should be dedicated. Corporate governance standards call for ethical conduct, also in the negotiation process. An ethical approach is more than just a courtesy granted to your negotiation partner. It is a gesture towards yourself. Eventually, you become how you treat other people. It goes without saying that the standards in this regard should be high. A goal should be rewarding for the two negotiators, both on the operational and personal level. Both parties should feel like the agreement crowns their mutual efforts, and that it makes them leave the negotiation feeling as more worthy individuals. A rewarding goal is the ultimate boost for the delicate ego.

Targets should be written down, so they can serve as a point of reference throughout the negotiation. The written word has a strong impact on what we perceive as reality. Once something is written, it becomes legitimate, and hence non-negotiable. In terms of attributing values to the targets, imagine the negotiation as a picture frame. The borders of that picture are designated by the maximum (your aspirational value) and the minimum (the absolute must-have) that you need to obtain.

It is equally important to set a walk-away point. Often this part is omitted. Should this be the case, what will inevitably happen is that you will end up pushing your walk-away only to stay in the game. Eventually you might find that the final deal does not make much sense, because it is so far off from your initial goal. The frequently posed question is whether the walk-away is the same as the minimum. These two values should not be confused. The walk-away is 1 cent less than the minimum target. Learn to set it and be brave enough to leave the negotiation if you reach it. Walking away is extremely empowering. Try it out in a low-stakes negotiation first. Internally, it makes you realise that you can decide what works for you and reject anything that does not. Externally, it sends a strong signal to the other party. They imagine that you have alternatives, since you can afford yourself the luxury of walking away. Those who are perceived as having alternatives are already semi-winners. Setting high targets, often reflected in making an aggressive first offer, could also improve the final outcome.

Four things to take into account when establishing targets

1 **The number of targets** Although it is common to commit to multiple targets, management literature suggests that more than six targets attempted at once means that success is unlikely. Following many targets at once reduces the perceived importance of the individual targets.

2 **Target duration** Duration and time lapse have an impact on commitment. Many studies suggest setting relative short target durations, since commitment and enthusiasm are likely to decrease after six months.

3 **Size of the group involved in setting the target** The motivation and commitment also depend on the size of the groups that are implicated in setting the target. Smaller groups tend to have a higher individual involvement because of the greater association and responsibility lines.

4 **The source of the target** Credibility, legitimacy and trust of the source are key factors that can influence the commitment to the target.

Smarter negotiation target/goal template

SPECIFIC
- What do I want to achieve?
- By when do I need to close the deal?
- Why is this goal important? (Link the goal to the negotiation mission.)

MEASURABLE
- How will I measure the negotiation progress?
- What will be the key success factors?
- What benchmark will I use – the task or the relationship?

ATTAINABLE
- How will it be clear when the goal is attained – by signing an agreement, a memorandum of understanding, opening the door for future cooperation?
- Do we have enough resources (time, bargaining power, expertise, other) to reach our goal?
- Is it reasonable to assume that the target/goal can be reached?

RELEVANT
- Why is the deal important?
- Will it strengthen the partnership and/or the position of the organisation?
- What precedence will it create for future negotiations?

TIME-BOUND
- How long should the negotiation take?
- By when should the agreement be reached?
- Am I ready to start the negotiation now?

ETHICAL
- Can agreement be reached by ethical behaviours?
- Will the negotiation enhance the personal standards and corporate governance?

REWARDING
- Is the goal attainment related to my personal success or the overall organisational goals?
- How will it fulfil the negotiation mission?

Your turn to practice

Formulate a SMARTER target for your next negotiation. Indicate how the target will be:

Specific –

Measurable –

Attainable –

Relevant –

Time-bound –

Ethical –

Rewarding –

Common challenges of goal setting

Once goals are set, they are not carved in stone. Although their purpose is to lead you to your desired prize, some goals may need to be re-defined in the negotiation process. To overcome the challenges related to goals, it may be helpful to test the assumptions that served as the basis for setting the goals in the first place. The negotiation frame that you designate by the maximum and the minimum target should leave a margin of flexibility for the unknown that can surface when the rubber meets the road. Some negotiators are of the opinion that setting goals can potentially do more harm than good. To mitigate this risk, the following four points need to be considered when engaging in goal setting.

1   Losing sight of the big picture: goals tend to direct our attention to the realisation of a specific task. This close focus can cause us to lose sight of other important issues, such as long-term goals, or the relational aspects of the negotiation.

2   Increase in taking risks: challenging goals can encourage risky behaviours, such as making large demands that can forego value creation or destroy the relationship between parties.

3   Unethical behaviour: setting high goals focuses the attention on end results rather than the means of getting there. An extreme variation is the Machiavelli approach, according to which the end justifies the means. The risk is the emergence of an organisational climate that allows unlawful and immoral behaviour, such as cheating, lying or making false promises to the counterparty to reach the goal. Furthermore, negotiators who fail to achieve their goals might manipulate the negotiation results to hide their shortcomings.

4   Not learning from past mistakes and failing to cooperate: a narrow focus on goals may distract negotiators from absorbing broader lessons for the future. It may incite the adoption of competitive rather than cooperative and integrative strategies. This could lead to missing out on opportunities to create future value for the organisation.

Expert view

Tania Micki
CFO at Tecan, Switzerland

The main challenge related to setting goals is related to lack in a broad sense: lack of preparation, understanding, time, patience and asymmetry of information. I recall one situation when I was negotiating settlement terms in a high-stakes negotiation. We were progressing well, but at one point the discussion was blocked over something not very important. I tried to understand and get to the bottom of what was causing the blockage. It turned out that the other party had not signed the agreement with their own customer, so they could not sign off with us. Equipping myself with this information allowed us to proceed and for me to get what I wanted.

Another challenge is the intercultural factor. Depending on the culture, the approach to negotiations can be very different. You may need to calibrate your goal to the cultural context. You need to put yourself in the shoes of the other party and sometimes re-evaluate what is acceptable to give away in terms of your own goals.

You also need to know how to set clear boundaries of what is acceptable from the paradigm of your culture, for example know how to avoid bribery when dealing with partners from different cultural, ethical and legal backgrounds.

One of the modern challenges is the COVID-19 situation. The switch to virtual negotiations has made it more difficult to build rapport between the negotiation parties. Consequently, the negotiation process has become more goal-oriented and less relationship-focused. Finally, you cannot be too nice, otherwise others might step over your goals.

How we usually undermine our goals

Goals tend to be based on past performance, therefore new ones are usually set higher than before. This can hinder achievement since circumstances will change and it may be much more difficult to achieve higher results under the new conditions. Having successfully completed a difficult negotiation we might feel overly confident and aim too high in the next negotiation. Success is directly correlated to risk-taking behaviours. Those who ride the wave of success can take too many risks and jeopardise the chances for another successful outcome. Some targets are based on the wrong performance measures, such as only hitting the target price but damaging the relationship in the process. Goals are only communicated to those who are responsible for them with no 'ownership' or relation to the goal. Individual (and organisational) goals of both negotiators should be entwined with each other to create an interdependency bubble within which both parties operate. In such conditions goal attainment is dependent on the smooth cooperation between both parties – I need you and you need me to win.

Defining goals and targets is frequently used as a technique to enhance motivation. Both can help focus managerial action and encourage people to succeed in the realisation of the negotiation mission and enhance overall performance. Consequently, setting the right targets in high-stakes negotiations has become a critical issue for many organisations.

Summary of key take-aways

1   A goal is a broad statement of where you want to end up; targets help measure the extent to which you achieved your end state.

2   Do not enter in a negotiation without knowing what your goal is.

3   The goal should address both the task and the relationship-orientation (T + R).

4   Set challenging goals for yourself; however, once you obtain them, do not make the other party feel like a loser.

5   Be ready to re-evaluate your goals and walk away if the context changes to the extent that your overall goal cannot be met.

Further reading

1   Cranfield School of Management (2012) *How to Set the Right Performance Targets: A Ten Step Target Setting Tool.* Cranfield School of Management.

2   Doran, G.T. (1981) There's a S.M.A.R.T. way to write management's goals and objectives. *Management Review,* 70 (11): 35–36. See https://www.sft-framework.org/steps/targets-and-indicators

3   Lai, L., Bowles, H.R. and Babcock, L. (2013) Social costs of setting high aspirations in competitive negotiation. *Negotiation and Conflict Management Research* 6 (1).

4   Narayanan, J., Joshi, A. and Lavanchy, M. (2018) *The Art and Science of Negotiation.* International Institute for Management Development.

5   Ordonez, L.D., Schweitzer, M.E., Galinsky, A.D., Bazerman, M.H., Locke, E.A. and Latham, G.P. (2013) Goals gone wild: the systematic side effects of over-prescribing goal setting. *New Developments in Goal Setting and Task Performance.* Routledge.

CHAPTER 4
ESTABLISHING THE
OBJECTIVE

'Know what your objective is. Anything that does not contribute to
that objective is unnecessary; let those things go.'

Richelle E. Goodrich

What you will discover in this chapter:

- What a negotiation objective is and why it's important to have one
- Roadmap for defining the objective
- How to overcome the main challenges related to defining the objective

How to distinguish a negotiation mission statement from an objective

One of the challenges that business professionals face in their negotiations concerns the correct identification of an objective in a High-Impact negotiation. It is often mistaken with a mission statement or a goal. Even in negotiation simulations performed during training sessions, it takes the negotiation teams a lot of time to come up with an objective for their mock case. Many do not succeed in differentiating between the different concepts. The following is an extract from a negotiation involving a sale and purchase agreement, which illustrates the confusion:

'Our mission statement:

Support of the client in the drafting and negotiation of the company sale and purchase agreement taking into consideration the results of the due diligence'.

Now here comes the dilemma: Is this a negotiation mission statement, a goal or an objective formulation? *Hint*: do not let the heading that was proposed confuse you.

The purpose of a mission is to announce exactly where you are heading, both internally and externally. Values depict those behaviours and actions that will help get you there. A negotiation mission statement should answer the question: *How will we win?* – by means of which strategic moves and according to which values? Therefore, we can now eliminate the option of the example being a mission statement, since it does not indicate the strategic nor value-oriented *how*. This leaves two possibilities: the statement being either a goal or an objective.

A goal is the final destination where we want the negotiation to lead to. There are three driving forces on that journey: the individual governed by their motives and a multitude of emotions, the task that needs to be achieved (making a deal) and the relationship between the parties (the partnership). A properly defined goal will allow for a purposeful discussion that embraces all these three factors. We can now see that the option of the statement being a goal can also be crossed out. A goal in this case would be the sale and purchase agreement as the final end result. This leaves the objective as the only remaining (and valid) choice.

What is a negotiation objective?

The purpose of a negotiation objective is to answer the question: *What for?* It allows the negotiator to identify the purpose of the final goal that they have defined. 'What is your goal?' and 'What is your objective?' are two questions that test the different motives. An objective can serve as a screentest for the goal. It will force you to stop and think whether the negotiation journey is worth the effort. A goal with no supporting objective behind it can be just as alluring as a sirens call, and equally misleading.

An objective consists of a set of parameters upon which a satisfactory agreement is based. The parameters define the limits of acceptability of the final agreement. In mathematics parameters are constants in equations. So, in a negotiation we can set a sum of parameters that will define what is considered a successful outcome in terms of the achievement of the goal. Using the above example of a sales and purchase agreement we could imagine the parameters as follows:

Parameters of the buyer:

- Swift transfer of ownership
- Securing a low purchase price
- Limiting risk
- Obtaining protection for the asset
- Access to complete information about the asset
- Adequate quality of the purchased asset

Parameters of the seller:

- Getting the best purchase price
- Limiting liability or risk of exposure
- No liability outside of the contract
- Speed of transaction

Each party would then decide which sum of the parameters makes for an acceptable end result.

What is the correlation between a goal and an objective?

A high-stakes negotiation is like a game of chess. If you want to win, you need to plan a few steps ahead. In order to make a good opening move, you need to know what your goal and objectives are. Only those who know what they are going in for can get their pieces in a winning position. Let us now break down a job negotiation into a goal and an objective with its parameters to see how this can be applied in practice. For the sake of practice, let us assume that your negotiation goal is to land a job. All your efforts throughout the application and interview process would be directed towards getting the job. Many job applicants stop their preparation at this point. They fail to pose the question '*What for?*'. This question would indicate the objective with its different parameters. Let us assume that the objective would be for career advancement. This answer would then allow for distinguishing the supporting parameters from those that do not serve the objective. This could look as shown in Figure 4.1.

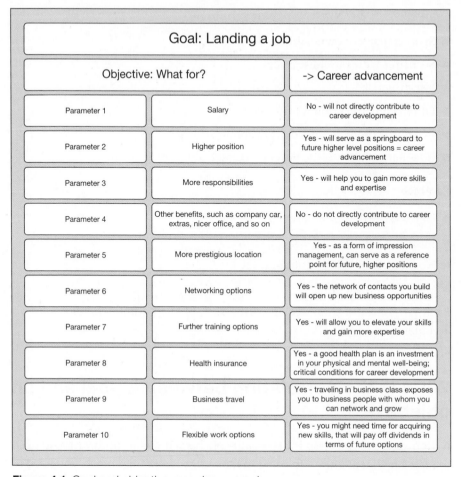

Figure 4.1 Goal and objective mapping example

The visualisation of the goal, objective and different parameters makes it easier to assess which parameters (or sum of parameters) related to the job offering will best serve the objective and make pursuing the goal worthwhile. In high-stakes negotiations it is recommended to break down the goal in writing. A systematic approach will allow for negotiation with a clarity of purpose.

Furthermore, approaching a negotiation with a set of objectives instead of focusing on a single inflexible objective, as well as a clearly defined range of agreement points are important strategic skills for any negotiator. Defining the objective and developing the parameters keep the negotiation focused on the desired goal. The nature of the negotiation is the reference point for both goal setting and defining the negotiation objective. Regardless of whether you are handling a one-off transaction or engaging in a long-term partnership, it pays off to take your objectives and those of the other party into account. A win–win between both objectives is a myth. Something will have to give. The parameter approach can be applied to eliminate the parameters that do not support your objective and to use those to make concessions (gives to the other party).

Expert view

Jonathan Faust
SVP/Global Controller at HP Inc., USA

It's important to first understand what exactly a negotiation is: a discussion between two or more parties who are looking to come to an agreement on a given matter in which they all have a vested interest. It's also important to understand if the negotiation is one-time in nature or will lay the foundation for future negotiations and/or a partnership of sorts. In either scenario, as one of the parties involved, you should take the time to determine what the other parties' objectives and points of view on the matter are. That will not only help you to negotiate more effectively, it will also enable you to maintain a better relationship with the other parties involved, which is incredibly important for anything that extends beyond being one-time in nature.

You should also be clear on what your objectives are. In most negotiation scenarios, you'll have more than one, or at least primary and secondary objectives. Ideally, you'd negotiate a perfect scenario and achieve all of your objectives, but you shouldn't expect that to happen every time. In most scenarios, you'll need to concede something that the other parties want. This is why it's so important to be clear on what your objectives are, and also those of the other parties in involved, so that you can propose trade-offs as necessary. Once you've done that, you'll have a better sense of the negotiation landscape, and can begin to formulate your negotiation strategy, working to protect the objectives that are more important to you, while conceding others, working your way to close the overall agreement in a manner that is the most favourable and acceptable to you as possible.

If you're looking to establish a successful, long-term partnership, you shouldn't try to achieve a lopsided win. If the other parties feel slighted, it will ultimately put unneeded strain on the relationship. In this type of situation, all parties should try to achieve a fair and balanced outcome, which means all will need to compromise to some degree. This is why having a deep and detailed understanding of the objectives involved is so important.

Roadmap for defining the objective

The definition of an objective is a two-way street. Both negotiators will have their goals. Consequently, the preparation of the objective should be performed according to the 'T-account' rule. In accounting, a T-account is an informal name for double-entry bookkeeping. It is designated with the letter T, because the entries (of credits and debits) are made in the layout that resemble a T. The logic for visualising the objective is similar. One side of the T-equation concerns your objectives, and the other side involves the anticipation of the objectives of your negotiation partner. In a high-stakes negotiation, the parties often run the risk of one-sided focus. Each party has their own goal, objective and a set of parameters. Naturally, these tend to be personal and thus subjective. As a result, it may be difficult to assess the situation from the perspective of the other party. Business professionals usually refer to this as, 'stepping in the shoes of another person'. Too often this turns out to be an empty phrase.

Five key questions to help you define your negotiation objective:

1 **What do I want to achieve?** Define a clear objective and outline the most favourable negotiation outcome and the least favourable terms that you are willing to accept to fulfil your objective.

2 **Why is this important for you?** Understand what you are in the game for and what are the motives driving your behaviour. Relevance is what will keep you going when the negotiation gets tough.

3 **Is there a fit between your objective and the type of negotiation?** Consider the nature of the deal (strategic vs non-strategic). For strategic (long-term or high-stakes) deals, you can accept less favourable parameters than for non-strategic (short-term or low-stakes) ones.

4 **Which parameters are you willing to sacrifice?** Specify which elements are critical for you and which ones you are willing to forego to achieve your objective.

5 **How will your objective impact the other party?** Look beyond the short-term outcome and foresee what are the long-term consequences of the

▶

objective you set. For example, a win where the other party feels taken advantage of will jeopardise the chances of implementing the deal and you reaching your objective.

Important note: These same questions should be used to anticipate the negotiation objective of the other party.

Main challenges related to defining the objective

The action of a negotiator is centred around a goal, while the objective is what gives meaning to that goal. Since a negotiation is based both on cooperation between the parties and interdependence of each negotiator, each one can block the other from attaining their objective. After all, a negotiation is not an exercise in philanthropy and both parties will be primarily self-interest driven.

The practical dilemma is that an objective is not always fixed logically due to the opportunistic nature of a negotiation. This can lead negotiators to use the wrong strategy in order to try and realise their ideal outcome, with no regard to the common objective. An interesting example are the Palestinian–Israeli negotiations. Some sources point out that these so-called peace negotiations are an Israeli objective, and that the negotiation objectives are only for show so that they can execute their own political agenda.

This brings up the question of whether displayed objectives are genuine in negotiations in general. Sometimes the negotiator does not even realise what their own objective is. I recall one interesting case where a candidate was negotiating a job at the European Commission. His goal was to get work for one of the European Union institutions. The procedure was complex, competitive and lengthy. The first phase involved pre-selection, where approximately 1000 applications for one position were collected and reviewed. The screening process eliminated approximately 700 applications that did not fulfil the job description requirements. The remaining candidates were invited to take verbal and numerical skills, abstract reasoning and situational judgement tests. This cut down the pool to approximately 100 applicants who were then invited to panel interviews. The panel discussions were conducted virtually with the Selection Committee members who were based in Brussels, Belgium. The candidates were invited to EU test centres all across the globe. During the virtual discussions, many technical questions were asked, practical knowledge about the EU was tested, there were case studies and other types of on-the-job activities. The pressure was high. Apart from these standard selection tools, the candidates were exposed to an array of tough negotiation and psychological tactics designed to test their mental stamina, resilience and reactions to stress. That eliminated the group to six legitimate candidates.

This particular candidate found himself among the selected ones. He was quite enjoying 'the EU jump-racing game' as he referred to the process. Passing the phases was amusing for him and even more satisfying for his ego. The challenge he set for himself kept him in the game for a total of eight months, the total duration of the process. Eventually, he achieved his goal and was offered a job at the European Commission. Then something interested happened: when the employment offer was presented to him, he no longer felt the same motivation he experienced during the recruitment. He ended up rejecting the job three days later.

This is what can happen when a negotiator sets a goal but fails to define the objective. Working at the EU level might have seemed alluring as a distant end goal, but the *'What for?'* question was addressed too late. Had the candidate investigated the reasons behind his goal at the offset, he might have realised that the lofty goal will quickly lose its appeal once it becomes reality.

How to overcome the challenges related to defining the objective

A remedy that can help overcome the challenge related to defining the objective is the popular managerial tool created by Peter F. Drucker in 1954, known as management by objectives (MBO). MBO is an approach that integrates organisational goals such as earning, growing and development with the individual needs of managers. Through the process the objectives of an organisation are converted into individual ones.

MBO is a modern method often used in performance appraisal to assess whether the employee has fulfilled the objectives set forth for them. As such, it introduces an outlook which is oriented towards the future. Many managers claim that MBO is the most successful method for performance appraisal. According to MBO, setting the objectives is part of the planning process and follows after defining the problem and setting a specific goal. The manager is responsible for giving specific instructions, setting quality standards and determining the time frame in which these objectives should be attained. The systems objectives should be compatible, clear and acceptable, which increases the chances of a successful outcome.

The aim of setting objectives is to know:

- what needs to be done
- when it is considered to be done
- that it is possible to do it
- why it needs to be done (and for whom)
- what the progress is.

The MBO model was designed to boost organisational performance by establishing objectives that both management and employees can agree to. The aim was for employees to have a say in the goal setting and plan execution. Creating a sense of ownership enhances commitment to the goal. The same approach can be adopted in high-stakes negotiations to align the individual goals of the negotiators with the common negotiation goal that has brought them together.

Summary of key take-aways

1   A negotiation objective identifies the purpose of the negotiation goal.

2   Use the *What for?* question to test your motives.

3   Prepare a set of parameters for your objective.

4   Distinguish the supporting parameters and eliminate those that do not serve your objective.

5   Build a bridge between your objectives and the objectives of the other party to create commitment to the end goal.

Further reading

1   Alavoine, C. (2012) You can't always get what you want: Strategic issues in negotiation. *Social and Behavioral Sciences* 58, 665–672.

2   Armstrong, M. (2009) *Armstrong's Handbook of Human Resource Management Practice*, 11th edn. Kogan Page.

3   Chamberlin, J. (2011) Who put the 'ART' in SMART Goals. *Management Services* 55 (3), 22–27.

4   Di Nitto, E., Di Penta, M., Gambi, A., Ripa, G., Villani, M.L., Krämer, B., Lin K.-J. and Narasimhan, P. (Eds) (2007) *Negotiation of Service Level Agreements: An Architecture and a Search-Based Approach*. ICSOC 2007, LNCS 4749, pp. 295–306. Berlin Heidelberg: Springer-Verlag.

5   Drucker, P.F (1954) *The Practice of Management. A Study of the Most Important Function in America Society*. Harper & Brothers.

6   Islami, X., Mulolli, E. and Mustafa, N. (2018) Using management by objectives as a performance appraisal tool for employee satisfaction. *Future Business Journal* 4 (2018), 94–108.

7   Koskinen, K.U. and Mäkinen, S. (2009) Role of boundary objects in negotiations of project contracts. *International Journal of Project Management* 27 (2009), 31–38.

CHAPTER 5
GATHERING THE NECESSARY INFORMATION

'Opinion is usually something which people have when they lack comprehensive information.'

Idries Shah

What you will discover in this chapter:

- Why it is important to equip yourself with information and what to look for
- The asking–listening–verifying (A–L–V) approach
- Information collecting cheat sheet

What is the purpose of gathering information?

Intelligence gathering aims at minimising the information asymmetry between you and your negotiation partner. The more you know about the other party, the better prepared you will be to lead the discussion from a position of power. You should enter the discussion only when you have equipped yourself with enough information to understand the person and their environmental context. Both factors will shape their negotiation objectives. Consequently, data collection and processing are performed on two levels: environment-oriented and person-centred.

The environment-oriented approach aims at collecting all the relevant information about the organisational landscape of the counterpart that may have an impact on their behaviour in the negotiation. The individual is always affected by the situational context within which they operate. Therefore, the more you know about their professional circumstances, the better equipped you will be to handle the person.

Gathering information about the environment

In the era of information overload, it is helpful to have a framework for information screening. The Environmental Check Tool will help you structure your search. The steps are as follows.

1   Go to the company website and look for the mission statement.

2   Identify which values are communicated. This will allow you a glimpse into the organisational culture of the firm. It usually has an impact on the culture of the individuals who work at the firm, including your negotiation partner.

3   See if you can find a negotiation mission statement – as we have seen, this is not a common practice. It is worth looking for articles about the firm's negotiation strategy on the internet. The person designated as the negotiator is an agent working on behalf of the firm. To some extent, they will be bound by the mission statement.

4   Do an internet search. Look for any recent news items about the company and its employees (perhaps you will uncover something about the other negotiator), opinions expressed by others, press releases, storylines and so on. You will gain more objective insights, other than the official ones that the firm wants to showcase.

5   Look for any existing opinions about the company and/or feedback from the customers. In most cases, these can be found by performing an internet search. Type in the company name and 'reviews or customer reviews/ opinions'. Although this may not be the most reliable source, you can see whether there are any common issues that are raised.

6   If the company is publicly listed, you can access their financial records to assess their financial health. This will help you understand how strong they are.

7 Check the number of employees, whether they have global presence, where their headquarters are. A family business with one office and a few employees will differ in business style from a multinational firm.

8 Perform a market analysis to identify the direct competitors of the company. You could consider them as your negotiation option B.

9 Find a contact person from inside the company, or a former employee, and have an open chat about the firm with them. They might be in possession of more detailed information about your negotiation partner and their circumstances.

Note of caution: Never rely on external information only. See if you can find any trustworthy internal informants that could equip you with more insights and confirm the accuracy of the assumptions you have made. Make sure you double-check that the information you possess comes from a reliable well. It is not uncommon for fake news to be spread in high-stakes negotiation to derail you from your track.

Expert view

Michèle Ollier
Co-Founder and Partner at Medicxi, Switzerland

Our company creates and invests in financial opportunities for start-ups in the life sciences sector. There are three main situations in which we engage in high-stakes negotiations: we negotiate to make an investment in a start-up company, we negotiate with external companies that could potentially invest in or do a deal with one of our start-ups, and when we want to hire key executives and new talent. As a first step, we need to make sure that we have the right program. We look at who could be the best partner for our company and who might be interested in its specific technology. Once we identify this, we then need to equip ourselves with the following information:

● Is it the right time for the venture capitalist?

● Have they recently done something that can be considered as competitive?

● What is the stage of development that they like to invest at?

● Are we in their scope of focus?

● What specifically are they looking for?

▶

One of the key points that you need to take into account when you prepare for a high-stakes negotiation is knowing who is the right person to talk to and how to approach them. The final decision maker is the person you should be speaking to.

When you ask for something, you are automatically in a weaker position. When we enter the discussion, we therefore try to avoid requesting anything or placing our demands on the table. Instead, we try to design an environment where the other party needs something from us, or they see an interest in cooperating with us. The approach that might work is to discuss something related, position the other party and pitch them in a way that will be attractive to them. Don't go in if they are not interested. You need to carefully create the right environment before you enter the negotiation.

Gathering information about the negotiator (profiling)

Once the environment overview is done, it is time to proceed with a general analysis of the silhouette of the negotiator with whom you will be interacting. Start with a simple internet search, go on the website of your negotiation partner, then check their professional profile and find out if you can infiltrate their social networks. What people post, which topics they take interest in, who they follow, where and how they spend their time, and with whom they associate can reveal a lot about their individual preferences.

Profiling is the analysis of psychological characteristics performed in order to predict a person's behaviour and capabilities in a given situation. The origins of profiling go back to forensic psychology, but the approach is now also used in business interactions and corporate settings. The primary purpose of profiling is to predict how a negotiator will act in a given situation based on their psychological silhouette, their individual preferences and the circumstances that affect them.

Studies conducted at the Harvard Program on Negotiation define four basic personality profiles which may impact your negotiation style.

1 **Individualists** who mainly focus on maximising their own benefit and show little to no concern for the counterparts' outcome. They often tend to argue their positions forcefully and at times make threats.

These traits will help you understand whether you are dealing with an individualist:

- Self-confident
- Analytical
- Drives changes
- Methodological
- Independent.

2 **Cooperators** put their focus on maximising their own as well as their counterparts' results. They are more open to value-creating strategies, exchanging information and making multi-issue offers, more so than individualists.

These traits will help you understand whether you are dealing with a cooperator:

- Collaboration-oriented
- Empathetic
- Patient
- Friendly
- Supportive in group work.

3 **Competitives,** also referred to as venturers, are motivated by maximising the difference between their own and their counterparts' outcome. They tend to block collaborative solutions and rather engage in self-serving behaviour.

These traits will help you understand whether you are dealing with a competitive:

- Assertive
- Analytical
- Taking the lead
- Goal-oriented
- Tough minded.

4 **Altruists** are rather rare in negotiators, since they focus on maximising their counterparts' outcome rather than their own.

These traits will help you understand whether you are dealing with an altruist:

- Can be overly trusting
- Sociable
- Organised
- Precise
- Seeking harmony.

When gathering information about the person it is important to pay attention to the following elements:

- **Culture:** Culture may heavily impact our values and behavioural norms and those of your negotiation partner. It can also take other forms, including socio-economic, ethnic and religious. Identification of these different concepts can help overcome misunderstandings.

- **Intelligence (IQ and EQ):** Intelligence as measured with IQ scores can be a good predictor of success. Educational achievements can indicate intelligence and learning potential. Willingness to grow and learn are important in negotiations; however, they do not take into account interpersonal skills. Nowadays, emotional intelligence (EQ) and social empathy, understood as the ability to understand one's feelings and how they affect others, are equally important (if not more) than high IQ scores alone.

- **Personality:** A popular personality and easy-to-use assessment tool is the Myers–Briggs Type Indicator (MBTI). According to this typology, personality assessment can be sectioned into four main indicators which show two extremes of a given personality feature:

  - Extraversion – Introversion
  - Sensing – Intuition
  - Thinking – Feeling
  - Judging – Perceiving

Discover your personality type: Personality Test from https://www.humanmetrics.com

- **Motivation:** Motivation to negotiate can vary depending on internal factors rooted in the psyche. There are several areas in which negotiators' motivation may differ from each other irrespective of their negotiator profile:

1   According to Maslow's motivation theory, several needs affect us at any one time (physiological, safety, belonging, esteem, self-actualisation). By targeting unsatisfied needs, you can stimulate the desired behaviour.

2   People are driven by three different types of needs: power (the desire to influence others and events), affiliation (the desire to establish, maintain, and restore close personal relationships with others) or achievement (behaviours oriented towards competition and achieving excellence)

3   Motivation can be boosted by positive beliefs about winning the negotiation. It will also depend on the level of self-empowerment and confidence.

4   The personal stakes involved can stimulate performance, for example if the negotiation benefits you personally, you will be more motivated to negotiate better.

5   Motivation can also be reinforced by linking the direct results of performing a task – the first-level outcomes (for example, closing the deal) with second-level outcomes, which are the secondary effects that the first-level outcomes will produce (for example the feeling of victory and pride related to closing the deal).

There are many personality assessments and psychological traits tests. The presented slice of a very broad field of study aims to highlight the variety of angles that can impact profiling. It is worth noting that the purpose of all the existing classifications is to minimise subjectivity of judgements. While working with professionals I observe that the main challenge they face is to control the impulse to form immediate opinions. When they are asked to profile the negotiator with whom they will be dealing with, the profiling quickly spirals towards opinionated assessment. It is not uncommon for pejorative adjectives, stereotypes or generalisations to be used. Conclusions should only be drawn from observed behaviours, otherwise they risk reflecting personal biases.

Information collecting cheat sheet

- Perform an analysis of the external and internal background of your negotiation partner using the Environmental Check Tool.

- Verify the accuracy of the data you have collected by comparing it with different information sources, for example the internet, client reviews and internal information sources.

▶

- Identify which negotiator profile they are:

  - Individualist

  - Cooperative

  - Competitive

  - Altruist

  You can gather some of this information from introductory talks with your partner, by performing an internet check on them (you will find a lot of information looking at their social networks, what they post, which professional circles they join, who they follow) and by speaking with people who might know them or have negotiated with them in the past.

- Perform an MBTI test to understand your personality type. Knowing which type you are may help you spot differences and similarities between you and the other negotiator.

- Identify points of profile compatibility, in lack thereof consider appointing another negotiator. For example, an introverted person might have a difficult time negotiating with an extravert, a cooperative negotiator will clash with a competitive one.

Until you meet the person personally, either face-to-face or virtually, you are operating based on the assumptions you have made from the information you gathered. The Asking–Listening–Verifying (A–L–V) method will help you check the accuracy of the information you gathered. You can use it when you have a direct interaction with the other negotiator.

The A–L–V approach to information gathering

Asking

Simply asking can reveal a lot of information, yet many negotiators struggle with the way they express their questions in a collaborative way. Since negotiation is often viewed as a battle over a fixed pie, questions can be regarded with suspicion. The main difficulty lies in sharing a sufficient amount of information to uncover valuable trade-offs, but without disclosing information that can be used against you.

It is recommended to pose **open questions**. They tend to be perceived as more accommodating and they encourage a more detailed answer than a brief yes or no. Open questions usually begin with the words: *Who, Whose, What, When, Which* and *How*.

Be careful not to make the information gathering feel like an interrogation or accusation. Keep an open mind (and ear) at all times. It is best to assume you never know enough, and that you can always learn something new from the other person. This will motivate you to listen.

Use follow-up questions to keep the conversation going and the information flowing. Examples such as 'I see', 'What happened after that?', or 'Tell me more' exert subtle social pressure to respond in more detail. Using silence as a probe can also be helpful. Give the speaker time to reflect and choose their tempo. Do not rush, wait for an answer before you introduce the next question.

Some negotiators suggest slicing down the questions to only two: *What* and *How*. The *What* question will identify roadblocks (What is causing resistance of your negotiation partner?) and the *How* will point to a way to overcome barriers to agreement.

Summarising as well as asking for more clarifications or concerns that were not addressed yet can further encourage the counterpart to share more information. It is important to phrase questions in a neutral way without implying any judgement or preferences about what is wrong and what is right. This is perceived as less confrontational and increases the acceptance of further inquiries.

Listening

To overcome resistance, communicate a desire to gather information in order to achieve a mutual gain rather than a personal one. Place the emphasis on listening, not on talking. In a high-stakes negotiation, each negotiator feels that they need to defend their own interests. This can lead to a one-sided focus and unilateral solutions. To step out of that tunnel, refrain from presenting arguments in support of your logic. Listen to your negotiation partner, make them feel accepted and understood.

Verifying

When gathering information and interpreting the findings, it is very important to consider interpersonal differences. The different paradigms that govern our behaviour can make it more difficult to understand the other person's choices. Make sure to double-check the accuracy of the assumptions that you made. Verify that your comprehension is correct by checking back with your negotiation partner. On the strategic level, this will allow you to uncover information that you might have missed in the initial asking round. From the relational perspective, it will communicate to them that they are important to you, which in turn will lower resistance. Figure 5.1 presents a roadmap to collecting and systematising information before and during negotiation.

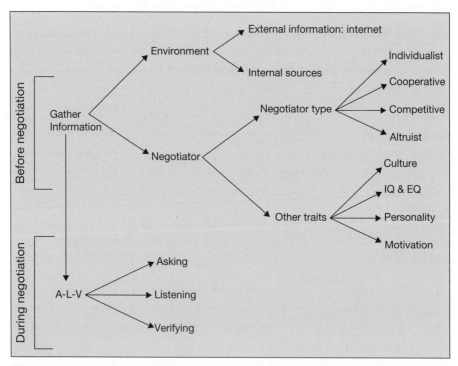

Figure 5.1 Information collecting map

Ethics-based approach to information gathering

Negotiation is not just a process, but above all, it is a human-to-human interaction. Each individual has their own particularities, preoccupations and interests at stake. Each negotiator has the right to respect and protection of their privacy. Information gathering should be performed in order to understand how to best approach the other person, not to humiliate or otherwise harm them. Transparency and honesty should be your guiding principles. Remember that you are equipping yourself with information to be able to build a partnership. Trust is critical. Be open about why you need information. Your credibility as a negotiator is on the line.

Summary of key take-aways

1 Equip yourself with all the necessary information before starting the negotiation.

2 Collect the data on two levels: environment-oriented and person-centred.

3 Apply the Asking–Listening–Verifying approach to information gathering.

4 Check the accuracy of the assumptions you made in the course of information gathering.

5 Find out what is important to the other party and design an environment where they need something from you.

The article 'Negotiation skills: time to ditch the winner-takes-all approach' by Gillian Ku presents the findings on how gender can impact ethics in negotiations.

Negotiation skills: time to ditch the winner-takes-all approach

By Gillian Ku

Financial Times, 28 March 2017

Negotiation stereotypes tend to celebrate a masculine, aggressive, winner-takes-all mentality, even when unethical actions are in play. These stereotypes are not constructive, but is there room for a more ethical style in today's uncertain world?

➡

Recent research that I carried out alongside Professor Jessica Kennedy (Owen Graduate School of Management) and Professor Laura J Kray (Haas School of Business) shows that women are more ethical than men when they negotiate. There is a 66 per cent probability that a woman will have a stronger moral identity than a man, according to our findings. That is, a woman is more likely to conceptualise herself in terms of moral traits such as fair, honest, generous and kind. In turn, when women are given negotiation responsibilities, they act more ethically. For example, we looked at people selling used cars – high-stakes negotiation with ample room for deception. We found that women were less likely to cognitively justify unethical actions to themselves and less likely to behave opportunistically than men because of their stronger moral identities. This contributes to our understanding of negotiation-related gender issues in the workplace, such as why women are paid less than men, and why there are fewer female leaders. It is a tragic truism that companies tend not to be gender balanced, and a company boss might ask, 'Why should I hire a female negotiator?' if they think a successful negotiation can only be achieved in a combative way. We hope our findings will start to change the way people think about good negotiations, shifting away from an aggressive mentality. The research has broader implications too. In the long run there may be negotiations, hopefully many, where it will be beneficial for men and women to be ethical. Not all negotiations are one-shot deals where you shake on it and walk away. Many, such as those with clients and suppliers, are merely the beginning of a long relationship. People want to know that they are dealing with a negotiator who is upstanding and trustworthy. In the long term, the aim is to make people aware that these harsh stereotypes around negotiations exist, that they exist on a very masculine level and are damaging. It is impossible to attempt to teach future business leaders how to be ethical in one classroom session, but business schools do have a responsibility to teach their students ethics. They also need to demonstrate that this style of negotiation does not necessarily result in good outcomes and could be harmful where long-term relationships need to be developed.

Further reading

1   Cambria, J. (2019) *Parliamone. L'ascolto, l'empatia, le parole giuste per negoziare con successo in qualunque situazion*. ROI Edizioni srl.

2   Elfenbein, H.A., Curhan, J.R., Baccaro, L., Eisenkraft, N. and Shirako, A. (2010) Bargaining behaviors. *Journal of Research in Personality*, May 2010.

3   PON Staff (2020) Identify Your Negotiation Style: Advanced Negotiation Strategies and Concepts. Understand your negotiation style to become a better negotiator. Negotiation Skills, from: 'Is Your Bargaining Style Holding

You Back?' First published in the Negotiation Briefings Newsletter, December 2009.

4   Scoular, A. (2011) *The Financial Times Guide to Business Coaching*, 2nd edn. Financial Times/Prentice Hall. (See Chapter 7: Deepening Coaching Skills: Working with Individual Differences.)

5   Taylor, J., Furnham, A. and Breeze, J. (2014) *Revealed: Using Remote Personality Profiling to Influence, Negotiate and Motivate*. Palgrave Macmillan.

6   Winerman, L. (2004) Criminal profiling: the reality behind the myth. *Monitor Staff* 35 (7).

CHAPTER 6
DECIDING THE BEST APPROACH FOR THE NEGOTIATION

'Success is 20% skills and 80% strategy. You might know how to succeed, but more importantly, what's your plan to succeed?'

Jim Rohn

What you will discover in this chapter:

- The six negotiation strategies and guidelines on how to determine which one to use

- The main factors to take into account when choosing the right strategy

- The importance of balancing the task and relationship (T + R)

The distributive and integrative approach – to divide the pie or make it bigger?

There are two main approaches to negotiation – distributive and integrative. The six negotiation strategies – competition, collaboration, compromise, avoidance, accommodation and hybrid – stem from this distinction. They will be discussed in more detail later in this chapter.

The **distributive approach, also called competitive, win–lose, zero sum or value claiming,** sees the object under negotiation as fixed. According to this logic, the more one of the parties wins, the less the other one will get. Consequently, a negotiator with a distributive mindset will try to maximise the benefits for himself and dominate the other party. Some negotiators may use force, power, or manipulation to reach their singularly focused goal.

The integrative approach, also referred to as collaborative, value creating or win–win, assumes the existence of variable amounts of resources. The assumption is that these can be divided and shared so that both parties can win, and the joint outcomes are maximised. This strategy relies on both parties' willingness to share information, cooperate and engage in mutual problem solving. Creating value, rather than a unilateral distribution of the resource, is the main goal. Figure 6.1 presents the two approaches and introduces the six negotiation strategies that will be discussed in more detail in this chapter.

Negotiation is an exchange between two parties trying to find an agreement that satisfies both their needs regarding the division of a limited resource (or perception of limitation of the resource). This perspective focuses on the specific task that both negotiators want to achieve. Assuming that negotiation is not only a transaction, but a human-to-human dynamic, what is missing here is the relational quotient. Both the distributive and integrative approaches primarily address the non-human factor, the task itself. The relationship element is omitted. The integrative attitude is more multidimensional, in the sense that it tries to expand not only the resource but also the value attributed to it. This is where things start getting interesting. Value is in the eye of the beholder.

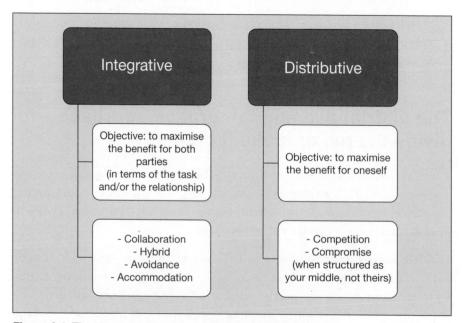

Figure 6.1 The six strategies on the integrative/distributive axis

What is valuable for one person may hold little to no meaning for another. The varying perceptions open the door for an exchange to happen. The best practice is to trade something of less value to oneself in return for something of more value, but with less weight for the other party. The interchange goes beyond the task itself. It relies on understanding the person behind the objective and uncovering their needs and desires. This is where the relational aspect gains importance. For both parties to openly share their motives, they need to expand their vision outside of the purely task-oriented focus. The investment is well worth the effort, since the end result may be the maximisation of the benefits flowing from the resource under division.

Therefore, **the condition for a sustainable and executable agreement is a balance between the task and the relationship** through the choice of strategy. What this means in practice is that both parties need to feel that they achieved or maximised their individual objectives, and that the relationship between them was preserved (ideally strengthened, and in no way ruined). On the task level it is recommended to bake a larger cake before splitting (distributing) it. By expanding the resource and reinforcing the relationship, both parties can have the cake and eat it, too. The balancing act between the task and relationship is presented in Figure 6.2.

An effective negotiator must be adept both with balancing the T & R as well as with applying both approaches. This means that you need to be ready to face a core strategic choice: when to focus on growing the pie and when to focus on dividing it. Here are three insights before we move on with discussing the six possible negotiation strategies.

- **Think big**: Diplomats are often very effective negotiators. A key factor in their success is the ability to enlarge their focus and think of the big picture. They have the ability to extract the important information, whereas other negotiators might fail at identifying this information and get lost in

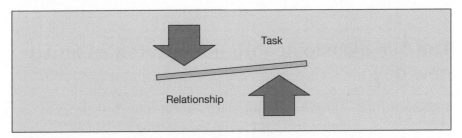

Figure 6.2 The task and relationship (T + R) balance

irrelevant details and data overflow. This ability to think big but in a focused manner is referred to as bounded awareness in negotiation.

- **Think ahead**: Skilled negotiators think several steps ahead. This skill can be learned by broadening the outlook and looking further than the immediate specifics of the situation. Each decision in a negotiation will be like a stone thrown in the lake. It will make small waves. Think what your actions will cause below the water's surface. For example, if you agree to offer a discount, you will be creating a future expectation that this will happen again.

- **Think broad**: An important issue in high-stakes negotiations is to take a larger view of the company's mission, rather than just focusing on the options existing at the moment of a specific negotiation. It is important to have a sense of the larger strategy and the direction where the negotiation should lead to before deciding on which strategy to adapt.

One of the negotiation myths is that only collaborative strategies can maximise joint outcomes. To challenge this view and better understand the relationship between negotiators' strategy choices and the resulting outcomes, an experiment was conducted among a group of 136 students (see Olekalns and Smith, 2002). In this experiment 27 dyads were instructed to bargain under individualistic instructions, and 34 were instructed to bargain under cooperative instructions. The individuals participated in a simulated five-issue negotiation. The study showed that negotiators were able to maximise joint gain under cooperative as well as individualistic orientations, but they achieved this in different ways. The conclusion was that optimum outcomes are a result of making multi-issue offers and the use of indirect information under an individualistic (competitive, distributive) orientation and applying reciprocity and the use of direct information under a cooperative (integrative) orientation. This experiment shows that the distributive and the integrative approaches can both lead to successful outcomes depending on the context and circumstances. The two approaches are the starting point for choosing the right negotiation strategy.

The five classic negotiation strategies and a new one

1 **Competition** – also known as distributive or win–lose. This strategy focuses mainly on satisfying your own needs and splitting the pie. As the name implies, there will be a winner and a loser.

When to compete: In one-off transactions, with low interest in or potential for a long-term partnership, or with a partner who refuses to collaborate.

2 **Collaboration** – the integrative or win–win strategy. It focuses on finding the best possible option for both parties and enlarging the pie with creative solutions. The standard understanding of a double win is not fully accurate. In order to achieve a real win–win outcome, both parties need to have a win–win mindset. A win–win will not be possible if one negotiator sees the negotiation as a win–lose situation. Therefore, it would be more fitting to refer to this approach as a triple win, which encompasses the individual negotiator`s mindset and then the win–win between both parties, as shown in Figure 6.3.

When to collaborate: In deals with an aspiration for longevity.

3 **Compromise** – a situation in which both parties win, and both lose something, so a simultaneous lose–win and a win–lose. In practice a compromise is sometimes confused with collaboration. The difference between these two strategies is that a win–win is achieved through concessions (giving something in exchange for receiving something), while a compromise is a result of a quick, non-creative division of a resource, for example meeting in the middle or a 50/50 split.

When to compromise: When a quick solution is needed and there is no time for creating options for mutual gain.

4 **Avoidance** – a standstill during which no action is taken. There is no exchange of value, and no concessions are made.

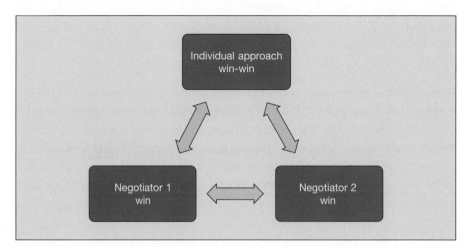

Figure 6.3 The triple-win approach

When to avoid: When emotions run high and a cool-off moment is needed to reconvene.

5   **Accommodation** – a strategy when one party yields and tries to satisfy the other parties' needs.

When to accommodate: When the relationship is more important than the task.

6   **Hybrid** – a mixture of all the five strategies.

The recommended path for incorporating all the five strategies by the hybrid is as follows: Start with competition to make your mark by entering the negotiation from a strong position of power. Be assertive about what you need, aim high. Then apply the avoidance strategy – back off, do not insist, do not pressure the other party. Leave them time and space to digest. In the meantime, you can accommodate by making small concessions. Give the other party something that has less value for you. This will show that you respect their needs too. Check their reaction. If there is reciprocity, you can make a small compromise. Then steer the dynamic towards collaboration.

The hybrid approach resembles the 'join up' technique introduced by Monty Roberts and made famous in his book '*The Man Who Listens to Horses*'. Roberts, known as the horse whisperer, revolutionised the method of training wild horses. Having spent years watching wild mustangs, he discovered their body language, ways in which they communicate with each other, how they behave, form hierarchies and establish relations among herd members. The fruit of these observations was the introduction of a new approach to breaking in these wild animals, without breaking their spirit. Roberts proved that power, force and pain were not the best tools for cooperation between man and animal. His method became widely popular and gained fans from all over the world, including Queen Elizabeth whose horses were trained by Roberts.

In the 'join up' technique, the trainer initially dominates the horse by chasing it around the round pen (with no direct body contact nor use of force). This goes on until the animal starts showing signs of acceptance of the person, such as lowering of the head, change of feet and body movement. At those signals the trainer tunes down the dominant behaviour and gives the animal time and space. It does not take long before the horse starts following the trainer around the pen.

Roberts observed that the key to working together is **reading body language, spotting the readiness to cooperate and respecting the autonomy** of the horse throughout the process.

The same principles can be applied in negotiations. A good negotiator can hear the ego speak; a great one can hear it whisper. Adapt the right strategy, and you can become the ego whisperer.

Negotiation is a fluctuating process. As such, there may be occasions when the approach of the other party changes. In such cases you might need to shift the strategy mid negotiation. An example on how to steer the negotiation from competition to collaboration is given below.

Example from practice

This is an email following an offer in response to a request for a proposal for a consulting mandate. You will notice that the strategy is reflected in the formulation. Words shape perception. Consequently, the way you structure your communication will have an impact on the recipient of the message and their reciprocal negotiation approach. The first message is crafted in a competitive manner, but the second one shows signs of willingness to collaborate.

I have briefly discussed your offering with our head of procurement and noticed that you applied the consulting daily rate and an additional 10% discount on this rate. To go ahead with your proposal, we need an additional 18% discount from you. Apart from this, we require ten (10) complimentary consultant hours. I am sure you understand the importance of this project for the future partnership.

Spotting collaboration potential (the specific elements are underlined and explained):

I have discussed your offering with our head of procurement and noticed that you applied the consulting daily rate and an additional 10% discount on this rate, for which we thank you. Is this your last offer or can you grant us 18% additional given the high order volume? Apart from this, would you be able to offer us ten (10) complimentary consultant hours? That would be highly appreciated given the importance of the project for our future partnership.

Indicators of willingness to collaborate

- Omission of *'briefly' discussed*, removal of the adjective that may cause the other party to think that the proposal was not worthy of a more detailed or lengthy discussion (implied meaning: unimportant, irrelevant, secondary).

- *Thank you* – recognition and gratitude or appreciation for the gesture.

- *Is this your last offer or can you. . .* – not demanding, instead asking in a polite manner, bringing in another option to the discussion.

- *Given the high order volume* – providing support for your demand. Word of caution: lengthy explanations may soften your request and make the other party doubt you deserve what you are asking for. Keep supporting statements short and sweet.

- *Would you be able to* – giving the other party a choice and autonomy.

- *I am sure you understand* vs *highly appreciated* – the former is patronising, the latter shows courtesy.

- *For our future partnership* – the key word here is 'our'. This creates a mutual system in which both parties are equal players.

- The second email cleverly bridges the task and the relationship. The negotiator clearly yet elegantly expresses what they need, without detriment to the relational aspect.

A few more examples of shifting strategies

Compromise – collaboration

The best example here is the negotiation urban tale of the two sisters fighting over one orange. Eventually they decided on a 50:50 split. Once they divided the fruit, it turned out that one sister wanted the juice, while the other was only interested in the peel to add flavour to a cake she wanted to bake. The moral of the story lies in the focus either on positions (the *'What do you want?'*) or on the motives (*Why do you want it?*). In order to gracefully shift from compromise to collaboration, it is helpful to uncover the underlying reasons why you and your negotiation partner want something. It may turn out that you can both have your cake and eat it too with a glass of orange juice on the side.

Avoidance – collaboration

The power of avoidance relies on loss aversion. By doing nothing, you indicate that you are not necessarily seeking closure nor pressuring the other party. This can raise the interest of your counterpart. The implicit warning of avoidance is that you might invest your energy elsewhere. The ultimate goal should nonetheless be to steer from avoidance to possible collaboration.

When to use which strategy – the task and relationship (T + R) balance

The guiding question in terms of strategy is output driven: what do you want to achieve? In order to answer this question and choose the corresponding strategy, three factors need to be taken into account: the nature of the negotiation (short vs long term), the stakes (the task aspect) and the impact on the relationship. The first factor follows a straightforward rule. For negotiations with a potential for longevity it is recommended to apply the collaborative over the purely competitive approach. As far as the other two factors are concerned, Figure 6.4 shows the balance between the task and the relationship with a plus (+) and a minus (–). These symbols and their impact on the two elements of the negotiation are explained in the following table.

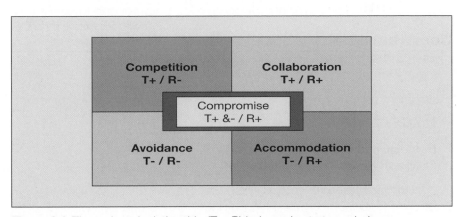

Figure 6.4 The task and relationship (T + R) balance in strategy choice

Adapted from: K. Jagodzinska (2020) *Negotiation Booster: The Ultimate Self-Empowerment Guide to High-Impact Negotiations*. New York: Business Expert Press.

Type of strategy	Impact on task	Impact on relationship
Competition – one party will win, the other one will lose.	The task of the winner will be maximised.	This may ruin the relationship between the parties. The loser loses face and may want to get even in the future. In some cases, this can jeopardise the implementation of the negotiated terms.
Collaboration – win–win for both parties	Both negotiators reach their objective.	The relationship is strengthened. The chances for successful implementation of the negotiated terms are increased and there is potential for future cooperation. There are no hard feelings.
Compromise – win–lose and lose–win for both parties	Both negotiators gain something at the expense of losing something else.	The task is partially achieved. The parties meet in the middle, and as such neither has the feeling that they have been won over. Word of caution: a compromise is usually their middle, not yours.
Avoidance – a temporary standstill	No active pursuit of the task. No negative or positive impact.	No negative or positive impact on the relationship. Cool-off period, which may be a test of the relationship.
Accommodation – a win–lose–win	Negative impact on the task fulfilment of the party who accommodates, in that sense a win–lose.	A positive impact on the relationship, therefore a win, because often if the negotiator chooses to accommodate, it means that the relationship is more important for them than the task.

Expert view

Dr Stephan Hartmann
Partner at Roland Berger, Switzerland

The main factor I take into account when I choose a strategy in high-stakes negotiations is the output. I ask myself: what do I want to get out of the negotiation process? The answer to this question will require an analysis of several other aspects.

▶

Firstly, I need to have a clear understanding of my negotiation power. Furthermore, I always make an assessment of my BATNA (Best Alternative to a Negotiated Agreement) – the best alternative(s). The choice of strategy will also depend on the level of complexity of the negotiation. I will use a different strategy for multidimensional deals, M&As, and restructuring than for simple negotiations. It is important to have a clear understanding of the positions. Depending on this assessment, I tailor my negotiation strategy. Going bullish can sometimes get you the optimal results, but it can also have a boomerang effect. That is why I always make sure to look out for the walk-away point of my counterpart.

To sum up, the three factors that I take into account are:

1 My negotiation power;

2 My BATNA (alternatives);

3 Clear understanding of positions: mine and theirs.

Clear understanding of these factors is the key. Setting the strategy is then a formalistic process that will hopefully lead to an optimal deal.

Summary of key take-aways

1 The choice of strategy is a balancing act between the task and the relationship.

2 Tailor the strategy to your desired output.

3 For long-term partnerships, apply the collaborative approach.

4 Follow the hybrid path: competition–avoidance–accommodation–compromise–collaboration.

5 You do not need to compromise the relationship to reach your objectives.

The article 'Compromise dies in the age of outrage' by Tim Harford gives an interesting outlook on negotiation strategies.

Compromise dies in the age of outrage

By Tim Harford

Financial Times, 31 May 2019

I don't often find myself agreeing with Esther McVey, but I wondered this week whether the candidate for leader of the UK Conservative party might accidentally have spoken the truth: 'People saying we need a Brexit policy to bring people together are misreading the situation. That is clearly not possible'. The British do indeed seem in no mood to compromise. The results of elections to the European Parliament produced a thunderous endorsement of parties that proudly reject an attempt to find common ground on Brexit. The Conservatives and Labour, each caught in an awkward straddle, were slaughtered. Labour offered the slogan 'let's bring our country together'. Ha! Voters preferred the Liberal Democrats ('Bollocks to Brexit') and the Brexit party ('they're absolutely terrified of us'). Sometimes an extreme position is the correct one. When King Solomon proposed cutting the baby in half, it wasn't because he was looking for the middle ground. Yet a capacity to find compromises is a good thing to have. Positions may differ, but whether we live in the same home or on the opposite side of the planet, we benefit when we can find a way to get along. If this new distaste for compromise is a problem, it is not the UK's alone. Positions seem to be hardening everywhere, the sclerotic arteries that may lead to a heart attack for western democracies. Perhaps this is driven by personalities. For a man whose name adorns a book titled *The Art of The Deal*, Donald Trump is curiously uninterested in negotiating lasting agreements with anyone. Or maybe it is a function of an information ecosystem in which outrage sells. Perhaps the problems themselves are more intractable. Some issues do not lend themselves to compromise. Brexit is one. Splitting the difference between Remainers and hard Brexiters is less like cutting a cake and more like splattering its ingredients everywhere. Egg on my face, flour on yours, and nobody even partially satisfied. Abortion is another. There is a principled case to be made for a woman's absolute right to control her body. There is also a principled case to be made for the absolute right to life of a foetus. But like the unstoppable cannonball and the immovable post, both rights cannot be absolute simultaneously. In contrast, other complex and emotive problems may still allow for compromise. On climate change, we can shrug and do nothing, or we can turn our economic system upside down, but there is plenty of middle ground between those options. In a trade negotiation, a mutually advantageous outcome is almost always there to be discovered. Roger Fisher and William Ury's classic negotiation handbook *Getting to Yes* advises: focus on the problem rather than the personalities; explore underlying interests rather than explicit positions; and consider options that may open up scope for mutual benefit. We may find a much better way to split the cake if we discover that you scrape the icing into the bin, while I would happily eat it with a spoon. It is sometimes astonishing how far a principled negotiation can go towards giving both sides what they want. It is clear that we British have failed to follow this advice. Our debate is driven by a bitter focus on personalities, from Theresa May to Nigel Farage to Jeremy Corbyn to the generic 'Remoaner elite'. Each side knows what the other wants but has shown very little interest in why they want it. Without sincerely exploring the underlying aims and values of warring tribes there is no chance of finding an outcome everyone can accept. The US debate also seems the antithesis of Fisher and Ury's advice. Too many politically active people seek the humiliation of the other tribe. Dismissing compromise as craven appeasement seems to be a winning tactic, particularly in the primary elections that set the tone of US politics. Compromise, however, is often possible even in unpromising situations. On abortion, for example, it emerges with a focus not on absolute rights but on practicalities. Many people can get behind policies to minimise unwanted pregnancies, and to make abortions safe and regulated rather than dangerous and illicit. It is a middle ground that many countries manage to find. One can see politics as a competitive sport or a search for solutions. There's truth in both views. However, a democratic election is far closer to a competition than to a principled negotiation. Do we not wish to see the opposite team soundly thrashed? Do we not boo their villainous antics and laugh at their mishaps? Who wants to play out a nil-nil draw? I would not want to venerate compromise as the supreme good in politics. Sometimes it really is true that you and I, dear reader, are absolutely right and they are absolutely wrong. (It may even be true that we are absolutely wrong and they are absolutely right.) Either way, the merits of the case must be weighed against the merits of trying to respect everyone. It feels good to win, but this isn't a fairytale: the losers won't stamp their feet and vanish through the floor. They – or we – aren't going anywhere.

Further reading

1   Bazerman, M.H. (2014) *The Power of Noticing: What the Best Leaders See.* Simon & Schuster.

2   Jagodzinska, K. (2020) *Negotiation Booster: The Ultimate Self-Empowerment Guide to High-Impact Negotiations.* New York: Business Expert Press.

3   Johnston, K. (2007) The art of haggling. *Business Research for Business Leaders* 7.05.2007.

4   Olekalns, M. and Smith, P.L. (2002) Testing the relationships among nego-
    tiators' motivational orientations, strategy choices, and outcomes. *Journal
    of Experimental Social Psychology*, 1 March 2002.

5   Roberts, M. (1996) *The Man Who Listens to Horses*. Arrow Books.

6   Shonk, K. (2016) Managing Cultural Differences: Negotiation Strategy and
    Diplomacy, Negotiation Strategy and Diplomacy in International Nego-
    tiations Dealing with Difficult People. Harvard Law School, Daily Blog,
    31.10.2016.

7   Trask, A. and Deguire, A. (2013) *Betting the Company*. Oxford University
    Press.

CHAPTER 7
NEGOTIATING VIRTUALLY

'It's not only moving that creates new starting points. Sometimes all it takes is a subtle shift in perspective, an opening of the mind, an intentional pause and reset, or a new route to start to see new options and new possibilities.'

Kristin Armstrong

What you will discover in this chapter:

- The key differences between face-to-face and virtual negotiations
- Practical tips for negotiating online
- How to choose the right medium for your negotiation

The 'new' normal or just a shift of perspective?

The outbreak of COVID-19 caused major disruptions across the globe. The pandemic crisis led to a worldwide tremor that affected the health sector, social ecosystem and the economic environment. The introduction of lockdowns forced business operations to go virtual overnight.

As well as COVID-19, increasing concerns about climate crisis might mean people choose to travel internationally less frequently. Consequently, professionals have to quickly learn how to operate in the new conditions with no adaptation period or any specific training. Negotiations have gone virtual. As the sphere that is often labelled as 'stressful, tense, or difficult', the additional emotional impact did not make things easier.

Although change is a constant, the uncertainty related to the new situation along with the confusion of changing rules and regulations made for a sensitive and stressful time. I experienced this feeling myself and saw it reflected in the behaviour of my business clients, training participants and students. At one point I even found myself pulled into the emotional spiral. This was not an ideal situation, since as a trainer and mentor I had to be the rock for my audience. After all, a successful negotiation starts with the management of oneself.

I remember the moment that was an eye-opener for me. It seems that the only thing that I was able to control during the pandemic was the progress of my book. I had a steady schedule of interviews lined up with negotiation experts who agreed to share their insights with me and my readers. One of these people was Agent Gary Noesner, the former chief of the Crisis Negotiation Unit at the FBI. During our virtual meeting, he said something that made me look at things from a different perspective. Agent Noesner said that most of the high-stakes negotiations that he conducted over the course of his 20+ year career were in fact virtual. In many of the interactions with kidnappers, hostage takers and law-abiding individuals, his only connection was a telephone line. The sentence that was a game changer for me was 'it made my ear focus more'. I found myself wondering what all the stress is about. After all, a virtual negotiation is nothing more than a shift of perspective with a strategic e-design. This thought was empowering because it allowed me to regain internal focus and a sense of control of the external negotiation environment.

Key differences between face-to-face (F2F) and virtual negotiations

The biggest advantage of e-negotiation is that it is quick and to the point. Operating in the virtual realm can reduce the time between the negotiation meetings and keep the dynamic swiftly moving forward. Due to the effect of anonymity, the virtual setting makes it easier for the parties to separate the negotiated issues from the personalities involved. Additionally, when nonverbal cues are removed, concession making and problem solving become the focal point, because there are less distractions related to decoding body language. In order to make the most out of the opportunities and benefits flowing from the e-space, it is essential to be aware of several factors that may hinder the virtual deal-making.

Establishing trust is more difficult

Apart from the obvious factor of physical proximity or lack thereof, the main difference between an F2F and a virtual negotiation lies outside of the tangible sphere. The key differentiating factor is related to bonding, and its most important effect – trust building. Trust is challenged in remote negotiations when presence and non-verbal communication are limited. The diminished ability to 'read the room' can lead to suspicion, perception errors and miscommunication.

Lack of direct contact breeds risk-aversion in the virtual setting. The dangers of being secretly recorded or listened to by another person who is offscreen are high since it is much easier to do this than in an F2F meeting. I have witnessed one negotiator break up the virtual discussion because they saw an elbow of someone who was not announced in the meeting. I do not recommend having incognito parties joining e-negotiations, but if for some reason you need to do that, make sure they lay low.

Less informal time

E-negotiations are characterised by a more linear and task-oriented approach. Consequently, the balance between the task and the relational components of the negotiation shifts towards the former. There is little pre-meeting interaction between parties and networking during breaks is limited. Negotiating virtually can leave parties feeling less warmth towards one another. All these aspects can adversely impact bonding during virtual meetings. To mitigate some of the risks, it is beneficial to have a well-planned negotiation strategy that includes adding the softer 'human' touch to the negotiation, for example by setting aside time and space for fostering trust. Schedule in time for small talk and non-negotiation-related exchanges. Anything that can replace the water cooler talks is welcome. Planning and alignment need to go beyond the scope of technicalities and strategic aspects. Empathy and emotional intelligence have never been more in vogue than they are now. In times of crisis, it is the ability to connect that can sometimes make or break the deal.

An integral part of business-making and F2F negotiations were small celebrations, such as luncheons, dinners or drinks that crowned the agreements reached. To ensure the same feeling of victory that brings the parties together after the ink has dried, you need to think about virtual substitutes and negotiation rituals. You can find out what your negotiation partner enjoys eating or drinking, send them a small gift of appreciation and set up an e-celebration to indulge in the treat through the screen.

Digital fatigue

Virtual meetings consume a lot of cognitive attention. Perhaps the most exhausting aspect of virtual negotiations is the digital fatigue. It is only partially linked to long hours of looking at a computer screen. The real problem is the self-focus triggered by having your own image in sight at every digital moment whenever your camera is on. The brain uses up a lot of energy by subconsciously checking yourself out. Taking selfies may seem like fun to some, but the perspective changes when the selfie mode becomes an integral part of the workday. It is as if we are negotiating holding up a mirror. The way that I avoid that when I conduct multiparty negotiations is by choosing a person with a pleasant facial expression and focusing my attention on their image instead of my own.

Lack of social cues

In a typical virtual negotiation, the computer camera angle reduces body gestures to the face/head, shoulders and hands (provided the camera is on). Therefore, misunderstanding and misinterpretation of signals may appear. As a result, participants are forced to make a greater effort in order to decode the verbal messages. This can be exhausting and demotivating. The fact that e-negotiations depersonalise the individuals (which is generally perceived as a setback) eliminates status differences, which in turn may lead to a greater sense of parity of power.

Studies show that female negotiators are less cooperative in virtual settings, whereas male negotiators' tactics do not change as much. The reason for this may be that when women detect less emotional cues, they feel less empathetic and less pressured to be cooperative or polite. Due to the lack of social cues in online negotiation, negotiators of both genders tend to engage more in bluffs, exaggerations and lies, which chip away at trust.

Intercultural differences

Cultural barriers can enhance the misunderstanding of objectives, messages and interests from the counterparts. However, people whose culture places more importance on individual rather than collective goals find it easier to switch to virtual meetings. Teams which are homogeneous (culture wise) experience less confusion and conflict due to communication issues during the virtual meetings. To break down cultural barriers, negotiators need to have more patience, respect and better listening skills.

Technological challenges

Technical difficulties will destabilise you and take focus away from the negotiation objective. Make sure that your software is updated and that the internet connection is reliable. Echo chambers, screen freezes and dropping off during virtual meetings do not convey an image of professionalism.

Among the most common challenges of e-negotiations are the following:

- internet connectivity and speed
- technology availability and use
- technology security
- time differences when negotiators are from different time zones
- confidentiality and privacy
- meeting length.

Based on research findings and my practice, I have not identified any solid evidence of superiority of the outcomes of an F2F negotiation over e-deals. The challenges of virtual interactions relate more to process management and design, which require a shift in both strategic and psychological approaches. The virtual tools will allow you to navigate the e-negotiation arena with more ease.

Practical tips for negotiating online

Here is a table that will make it easier for you to prepare and conduct e-negotiations.

Virtual negotiation checklist

Virtual tool	How to use it
● Agenda	The virtual agenda will allow you to control the time and flow of the process, as well as monitor progress. Present the agenda as a share-screen option. In terms of the agenda design, the same rules apply as in F2F negotiations.
● Documents arsenal	Have all necessary documents neatly organised and readily available, ideally in one folder.
● Setting design	Optimise your virtual setting: the framing, the lights and what others can see. Get rid of all distractions and limit the potential for interruptions. Make sure the background is neutral or serves the purpose you want to achieve, for example shows the logo of your company that you want the other party to remember.
● Seating arrangement	Where you sit and what you look at will have an impact on how you feel and what impression you make on the other party. Sit at a desk or stand at a worktable. Even if you are tempted to engage in negotiations sitting on the sofa or lying in bed, do not. Some people would never think of doing this, but others might. I have a recent example of someone who turned up to an important online meeting in what looked very much like a dressing gown. The relaxed setting and dress will make your deal-making mellow.
	What you choose to look at will impact your performance. For High-Impact interactions, place images of corresponding content in your direct environment.
● Virtual presence	Because computer cameras tend to be located at the top of the screen, when you look at your screen, you appear to be looking downward rather than at the person on the other end. Reduced virtual eye contact can impair negotiators from building trust and rapport. To manage this, move the square with your own image next to where the camera light is (top of your computer screen). The natural tendency to look at our own reflection will come across as if you are looking at the other party.
● Image design	Since all we can see on camera is the face, torso and hands, make sure that you are well groomed and properly dressed (at least to the waist). For those female negotiators who apply make-up, you might want to use a bit more; the camera makes your face look more 'naked'.
● Camera options	In order to avoid the 'now you see me, now you don't' game, invite all participants to turn their cameras on. Do this in a non-directive manner, for example by saying, 'I do not seem to see you' or 'I find it less effective to exchange with you when I do not see you', or 'Do not worry if it's a bad hair day, I don't mind'.

Virtual tool	How to use it
● Screensharing	Screensharing is a great tool for priming the other party to what you want them to see. The longer they look at the content on your screen, the more they will retain it. This is especially useful when you **present your demands**; keep them on the shared screen for as long as possible.
	Screensharing also takes the focus away from your face. If you are self-conscious, self-critical or camera shy, this is a great tool for making you feel more at ease.
	Use the screensharing option to draft up a **joint summary** of each meeting. By initiating the summary, you can control the content and verify whether you are on the same level of understanding. It is important that you make the other party feel like they are co-owners of the points incorporated in the summary.
● Role attribution	Assign clear roles. When you input names, do not use initials or numbers as these depersonalise. Include the organisational role of each person along with their name.
● Digital distractions	Schedule regular breaks to keep the attention span crisp and to avoid digital fatigue. Minimise any digital noise. Do not multitask. Focus on the other party, take notes and be present in the moment.
● Avatar communication	Control your facial expressions, your posture (at least the upper body), keep your hand gestures within the screen frame, pay attention to your para-verbal communication: tone, pitch, speed, intonation.
● Double-checking	Proofread your digital messages for the tone, send PDFs (Word or PowerPoint documents, disclose the modifications you made), check the attachments that you send. Be particularly careful which other content is visible when you share your screen.
● The good old phone call	Do not schedule a separate virtual meeting if what you need to say can be done over the phone. A virtual meeting invite obliges to fill up the meeting time (most platforms offer 30 minutes as the shortest timeframe). This time could be invested into moving the deal forward.
	In order to avoid getting caught up in the waiting game, agree on a response time at the start of the negotiation. By doing so, you will not have to wonder what the moments of silence mean.
● Prudence	Be very aware of the image you give through a video, in particular if not in a professional setting. Pay attention to what you say and share. You might be recorded without your knowledge or there may be other people listening in.

Choosing the right medium for your negotiation

The choice of medium depends on two factors: the individual preferences of the negotiator and the desired effect. You can select among oral (phone call), written (e-mail, instant messaging), visual (video-conferencing and online presentations) and electronic means. The characteristics of these media are presented in Figure 7.1.

Negotiators who are conflict averse tend to opt for non-confrontational modes of communication. Written media allow them to carefully plan and control the timing and content of their response. The downside is that the written channel makes it difficult to bond and explore the underlying interests of the other party. It may also send an implicit signal to the other party that you are building a record against them. Consequently, hiding behind e-mail or instant messaging can lead to parties getting stuck in their positions. I have often witnessed how a simple phone call can break the impasse of a week-long e-mail exchange. Verbal communication helps to convey emotions and minimises the risk of digital misunderstandings.

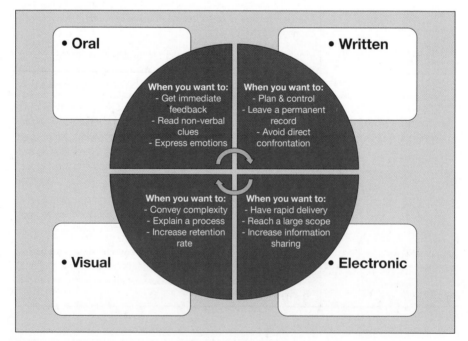

Figure 7.1 Choice of medium: when to use which?

Video-conferencing is by far the most interactive mode and the closest substitute to meeting in person. It is recommended to use technologies which resemble a face-to-face encounter most closely, such as Zoom, Webex, Google Meet, Microsoft Teams or Skype, with the camera on.

The choice of medium is driven by the cognitive preferences of the negotiators. People who are more analytical may be more receptive to visuals, such as diagrams, charts or graphs that can be used to convey processes and complex issues. Regardless of the negotiator profile, visual content is better retained than verbal messages. Words are easily forgotten; images are more difficult to be unseen. I strongly advise you to use visuals in the following situations:

● when you design and agree on the process together with the other party;

● when you present your demands (you should leave them in full view for as long as possible);

● when you jointly summarise the points that you agreed on.

Electronic media allow for rapid delivery and reaching a broader audience. The downside is that you lose control of the recipient pool. Make sure to plan your content and responses carefully.

Expert view

Fabienne Schlup-Hasselmann
Resposible for Projects Organisation at Cartier, Switzerland

The biggest advantage of written e-negotiations of commercial contracts is the time to check the accuracy of the terms, less of 'on the spot' improvisation as compared to face-to-face discussions, as well as the possibility to see the entire proposal at one's own pace before concentrating on the specifics. This asynchronous nature of electronic negotiations allows negotiators to capture the things between the lines and to get a better feeling of what is important for the other party.

In verbal e-negotiations the biggest advantage is the control over the environment (which can also be a challenge). Virtual meetings tend to be more focused. More negotiation points can be achieved in one meeting. The 'raise hand' option enables fluid communication, better transition between the negotiators and limited interruptions. Consequently, all voices can be heard; this is sometimes not the case in face-to-face negotiations when some people take over the negotiation and make it difficult for others to fully express their positions.

What I find particularly useful in the virtual setting is that you can see the names of the people involved in the discussion. In live meeting rooms you do not always have the name cards. Sometimes you do not know who all the players are. I would suggest adding the role to the name in the virtual setting to make the experience even better.

Summary of key take-aways

1 Virtual negotiation is nothing more than a shift of perspective with a strategic e-design.

2 When direct human contact is limited, the relational aspect needs to be even more strongly addressed in the negotiation process.

3 There is a richness of virtual tools to choose from. Use them to navigate the e-negotiation arena with more ease.

4 Minimise any potential sources of digital distractions.

5 Adapt the medium to negotiator preferences and the effect that you want to make.

Further reading

1 Carillo, K., Cachat-Rosset, G., Marsan, J., Saba, T. and Klarsfeld, A. (2020) Adjusting to epidemic-induced telework: empirical insights from teleworkers in France. *European Journal Information Systems* 30 (1). 19 October 2020.

2 Harkiolakis, N., Halkias, D. and Abadir, S. (2017) *e-Negotiations. Networking and Cross-Cultural Business Transactions*. Routledge.

3 Pinker, S. (2020) *The Science of Staying Connected*. WSJ Publishers, April 2020. See http://ilabs.uw.edu/sites/default/files/TheScienceofStayingConnected-WSJ_1.pdf

4 Vyas, L. and Butakhieo, N. (2020) The impact of working from home during Covid 19 on work and life domains: an exploratory study in Hong-Kong, PDP Singapore. 9 December 2020. *Policy Design and Practices* 4 (1). See https://www.tandfonline.com/doi/full/10.1080/25741292.2020.1863560?src=recsys

5 Waizenegger, L., McKenna, B., Cai, W. and Bendz, T. (2020) An affordance perspective of team collaboration and enforced working from home during Covid 19, Special section: Information Systems and Innovations in Public Sector. *European Journal of Information System* 29 (4). 12 August 2020. See https://www.tandfonline.com/doi/full/10.1080/0960085X.2020.1800417

PART 2
THE NEGOTIATION
PROCESS

CHAPTER 8
DESIGNING THE RIGHT ENVIRONMENT FOR THE NEGOTIATION

'I hope it is not a crime to laugh at all things, for I wish to know what, after all are all things, but a show.'

Byron's Don Juan

What you will discover in this chapter:

- The internal factors you need to take into account when organising the negotiation environment

- How to make the other party feel like they are involved in the process

- The techniques of external design: how to create a good setting and atmosphere

- For aspects related to virtual negotiations go to Chapter 7

The internal factors you need to take into account when you set the scene

In Part 1 we discovered the strategic blueprint for the negotiation process:

1 Defining the mission statement – answer to the *How will we win?* question;

2 Setting the goal – implementation of a concrete plan to fulfil the mission;

3 Establishing the objective – answer to the *What for?* question;

4 Gathering the necessary information – equipping yourself with information about the other party and their environment.

The next step in our journey is combining these aspects with interior (self-management) and exterior design (organising the negotiation environment).

Negotiation starts with you, specifically with your attitude. An attitude is a string of thoughts and feelings. Comparing this to negotiation, the thoughts are the logical, strategic elements and the feelings are the emotional, underlying factors. Thoughts shape the externalised strategic approach, while feelings fuel it from the inside. Therefore, the way you enter and lead a negotiation is a reflection of how powerful you feel on the inside. Many negotiations fail not because of a weak strategic approach, but due to a shaky inner construction that reveals itself in lack of conviction in one's own power and negotiation skills, and a disbelief that a win is possible.

Research and practice confirm that if there is a discrepancy between *what* you say (your verbalised message) and *how* you say it and *what* your body says (the para-verbal and non-verbal communication), the other party will believe the latter. The body is not a skilled liar. We can take this logic further. If there is a mismatch between the strategic blueprint and your attitude, the other party will surely pick up on the latter.

Self-Diagnosis

The best way for you to determine where you stand is to do a little association exercise.

For the following words write down your immediate connotations, the first thing that comes to your mind after you read each word. Do not analyse, it is important to grasp and note down your spontaneous instinctive reaction.

- Negotiation
- Win
- Partnership
- Stakes
- Competition
- Demands
- Conflict
- Agreement

▶

- Counterpart
- Compromise
- Deal.

Now take a look at your list. Which words prevail – those associated with a positive, powerful, mindful attitude, such as for example: negotiation – success, win–win, partnership – long lasting, and so on? It might happen that your connotations are less neutral or optimistic. If so, take a look to determine which of the words triggered more negative connotations. Is there a specific memory or experience behind them?

The first step to change and mental reinforcement is to understand what is causing a specific reaction. There might be factors in your consciousness, which you have pushed into the shadows of unconsciousness, that are holding you back from realising your full negotiation potential.

The next question is how to prime yourself internally for an external manifestation of power. Here are five helpful techniques.

1 **Failure is not an option mindset**: A frequent mistake made by negotiators is thinking that 'it's this deal or nothing'. This attitude, known as the knife on the throat, is a sure shot recipe for an emotional hostage-taking. By thinking you have no alternatives you become your own worst counterpart. Desperation is difficult to shake off and hide from the other party. When you go into a negotiation you should go in to win, not to minimise the loss.

   How to do this: Use the 'I will' formula. For example, I will win this deal.

   What to avoid : Phrases such as 'It would be nice to win', 'If only I could win', 'Maybe this time I can manage to win'.

2 **Enjoy the game**: Negotiation is not an exercise in philanthropy. It often is a way of resolving a conflict which involves making trade-offs. This is fascinating, because a conflict can have many positive aspects, depending on how it is managed. It can stimulate innovation and creativity in finding new solutions, it can create a system of interdependency between the two sides, or it can expand the field of vision beyond the obvious options.

   How to do this: Find out what the rules of the game are and become the best player.

What to avoid: Taking things personally. The other side is at the table to maximise the gains for themselves. So are you. Do not let them hold you back from reaching your goal.

3 **Relax, then negotiate**: Here is an interesting paradox that might help put things into perspective. Business professionals often share with me that they tense up before a negotiation, they dread what lies ahead, and wish it was over already. Meanwhile crisis negotiators from the FBI or the NYPD, who are involved in life and death negotiations, share with me that they face the crisis situations from a place of calm. Imagine how things would escalate if they added their distress to an already tense situation.

How to do this: Before the negotiation, listen to a song that calms you down or energises you in a positive way, or remember a joke that cracks you up.

What to avoid: The spiral of negativity and anxiety. Avoid people who usher you into any of these states.

4 **Beware of labels**: Imagination is often far worse than reality. This is what makes the mind the most dangerous place. The way that you paint the negotiation scene can become a self-fulfilling prophecy. If you brace yourself for a tough negotiation, it has just become ten times tougher, because you will pay more attention to the 'tough' aspects and sweep aside the positive elements (and vice versa).

How to do this: See a negotiation as any other life situation – it will have its ups and downs. Accept this and keep your eye on the prize when the going gets a bit tougher. It will then fluctuate back up. Nothing lasts forever, neither the good nor the bad moments.

What to avoid: Phrases such as 'this is going to be a difficult discussion', 'this is a high-pressure situation', 'I am entering a battlefield' (direct quotes from practice).

5 **Unique negotiation proposition (UNP)**: What is the one thing that makes you a great negotiator? What makes you stand out in comparison to your competitors? Identify what is unique about your negotiation style and why people want to negotiate with you. Business is usually personal.

How to do this: Identify the exclusivity of your offering. Are you skilled at listening to people, understanding them and their needs, communicating your demands, leading a negotiation, closing the deal, bridging the task and relational aspects, establishing partnerships?

What to avoid: Not knowing what your strong points are and instead focusing on your shortcomings. An extreme variation is accepting that you have no unique negotiation skills whatsoever.

One of my training participants once told me that she was always the most successful when she did not care too much about the outcome. Could a detached attitude be a secret recipe for deal-making? Certainly not by itself. 'Not caring too much' is a result of the following three conditions being met.

1 Instead of focusing on one outcome, try to keep your options open and consider at least two other offers. The knowledge of having other interesting options increases your power in negotiations and at the same time gives you the confidence to walk away when the offer at hand is not optimal.

2 Finding good alternatives will help you set up a plan B should the deal go south. This is called a BATNA – the Best Alternative to a Negotiated Agreement. If you decide to walk away from the negotiation, you can rely on your BATNA. In my view, BATNA crafting should be a perpetual process. The more alternatives you have, the less desperate you are for a particular deal.

3 The estimates of alternatives will give you an insight into the existing commonalities and differences between your needs and those of the other party. This will help you identify the 'trading zone' – the space where you can make concessions on differences to create value for both parties.

The three grand negotiation illusions

A skilled negotiator is like a magician. They direct the spotlight where they want you to look and they set the scene to create a desired effect. After reading Part I, you are well equipped as a strategist and ready to tackle the task-related aspects of the negotiation. However, a negotiation also consists of the relational factor. You are convincing your negotiation partner to your perspective and your vision. In that sense, negotiation is both art and science. Consequently, we now need to add a touch of art to the equation. Your role in this regard will be to create the three grand negotiation illusions for your negotiation partner. These are outlined below.

1 **Illusion of autonomy and choice**. The human psyche is made up of two elements – the ego and the self. Studies in analytical psychology show that the ego (the conscious) and the self (the unconscious) seldom agree as to

their preferences. The paradox of the individuation process lies in the fact that the separation of the ego from the self is a necessary condition for coming into maturity. This process occurs when we are about two years old. At that age, one of the strongest needs is to be autonomous (hence the period in the child's life referred to as the 'terrible twos'). It should not come as a surprise that your negotiation partner will exhibit this need. Nobody likes imposed solutions. The best way to respect the autonomy of your negotiation partner is to give them a choice. This does not mean that you completely hand over the reins. Instead, you should frame the choice. For example, if payment terms are one of the items on your demand list, but they are not a non-negotiable, you can frame this aspect as a choice. Would you prefer 30- or 40-day payment terms? Please notice that there is only 10 days difference between the two options. Nonetheless, it is their (illusionary) choice.

2   **Illusion of ownership.** I learned from my time in legal practice that a bullet-proof contract will in most cases be rejected by the client. Simply because it is not *theirs*. The chances of acceptance significantly increase when you involve the other party in the quest to finding a solution. An effective tactic is asking for their support or advice. This creates the sense that they were part of the end result. After all, going against one's own recommendations would be completely illogical. It is recommended to agree on the negotiation process together, before you each jump into the content. Most negotiators get this sequence wrong. Ownership is about getting the other parties buy in, having them feel that the agreement was reached mutually. This makes them more likely to stick with the agreement later.

3   **Illusion of victory.** If you ever put anything up for sale and it was immediately sold, you probably felt like you asked for too little. It made you question your judgement and cherish the deal less. Needless to say, you did not feel like you won. If you had the chance, you would probably take the deal back. This is exactly how your negotiation partner will think if you do your victory dance. They will become suspicious and they might even try to find a way out of the agreement. In order to avoid this, make them feel like they are victorious. You can do this by leaving a small concession for the end. Ideally, this should be something that has little value for you, but by them will be perceived as a token of appreciation and a sign that they also gained from the agreement.

Expert view

Sonalee Parekh
CFO at RingCentral, USA

The most important thing is to make sure that you understand the motivations of the other party at a deeper level. What drives their behaviour is more than just the financial aspect or strategic motivations. There is also the personal element, the underlying motives, sometimes the ego factor. You need to hear the other party out and uncover what they truly care about. You will need to do your homework – try to get as much information about them as possible, get into their head to see things from their perspective.

In high-stakes negotiations, you naturally want to get the best deal for yourself, but you also need to calibrate around what is a win for the other side. In order to achieve a mutually beneficial outcome, you need to be willing to give a little on the points that mean less to you. Don't expect to win on every point, that is a set-up-to-fail mindset. A successful agreement is one where both negotiators have made concessions, but they nonetheless walk away feeling like winners. Don't waste energy on things that will not move the needle.

A high-stakes deal is a package consisting of task and relational elements. You are selling your vision, and the other party needs to understand why they would want to close the deal with you and not your competitor.

When setting the scene for success, you need to think strategically, like a chess player does. Plan ahead. It takes a lot of work before you get to the negotiation table. The more complexity and variables there are, the more effort you will need to put in. Decision trees, talk tracks and rehearsals will help you prepare. Last but not least, assemble a strong negotiation team. Make sure you secure internal alignment, so that you enter the negotiation with conviction and from a position of power.

The techniques of external design

The physical space is an important aspect of the negotiation arena. The 2015 United Nations Climate Change Conference that took place in Paris can serve as a good example of what to pay attention to.

Create the right atmosphere: During the 18 months leading up to the conference, the French government designated a political agent to serve as a behind-the-scenes support in the discussions with fellow diplomats and academics. The aim was to instil urgency and optimism in delegates so that they could help negotiate the desired agreement. Laurence Tubiana, who was the chosen diplomat, was very detail-oriented when 'setting the stage'. With French flair, every workspace was softened by 'a gracefully curved table lamp, casting a gentle glow', then an onsite bakery was constructed to bring fresh baguettes and croissants. Adding to that, the negotiators had the chance to nap and refresh in relaxation rooms after marathon negotiation sessions. The environment heavily impacts mood and behaviour, and these small but significant changes promoted a calm and collegial negotiation space.

Partners, not advocates: Because of the disagreements between developing and developed nations, the task of leading the delegation was given to two chairs, namely Daniel Reifsnyder, from the US Department of State, and Ahmed Djoghlaf, an Algerian ambassador. The two had been working together for many years and complemented each other with knowledge and empathy. Instead of opting for lawyers and professional negotiators, the discussions were led by two representatives who had a track record for collaboration and even-handedness.

In high-stakes negotiations, it is recommended to engage an independent facilitator who can introduce ground rules as well as coordinate the conversation flow.

Getting on the same page: Almost a year before the start of the conference, a negotiation text was drafted by all parties and every delegate could propose anything they wanted. The purpose of this document was to build goodwill and trust. Such draft pre-agreements are often used in high-stakes negotiations to serve as a basis for collaboration. Furthermore, relevant issues and points of possible agreement can be identified.

Most successful negotiators consider the setting for a meeting to be a crucial factor. An old negotiation principle states: 'The better the mood, the better the agreement'. Hence it is important to create a pleasant atmosphere to make oneself and the other party feel comfortable. The following points can have a positive impact.

- **The venue:** When deciding upon the location, there are three possibilities: a neutral site, your partner's office (where they enjoy a psychological home advantage) or your office. To reduce the psychological disadvantage of your negotiation partner when inviting them to your office, follow these tips.

- Give your full attention and eliminate distractions such as phone calls and other interruptions.

- Have the meeting at a conference room rather than at your office to give your counterpart a feeling of equality.

- Do not make them wait. In many cultures this is perceived as placing yourself in the dominant position and showing the other 'their place'.

- **The time and length of the meeting:** One of the main challenges related to setting the stage for a successful negotiation is time. In high-stakes deals things move quickly and timing is not always in your control.

  The date for the meeting should be set in a way that neither of the parties feel external pressure regarding the time. Having multiple dates to choose from is ideal. The quality of the decisions made may suffer if a person is under time pressure. A part of the written invitation should include the start and end of the meeting and an agenda. Furthermore, complex negotiations should allow breaks for meals and refreshments.

- **The composition of the participants:** Negotiation is an interpersonal dynamic. The choice of the participants will impact the negotiation. To decide upon who to invite, the following questions should be considered.

  - Who has the mandate to negotiate?

  - Who has the power to make the final decision?

  - Are there any interpersonal dependencies?

  - Who will be seen as a credible authority?

  - What are the personality types and how will they interplay?

- **The agenda:** An agenda is one of the means through which you set the stage in a subtle and unimposing manner. It is necessary to distinguish between an introductory agenda (the invitation to start the negotiations) and the negotiation agenda. The former should be vague in terms of the content of the negotiation. There should be no demands communicated in advance; this will prevent your negotiation partner from preparing counter-demands ahead of the discussion. For example: 'We would like to discuss a potential partnership with you. We are inviting you to a 60-minute meeting on the...'.

  The negotiation agenda will be discussed in more detail in Chapter 11.

What you need to accomplish is to place yourself in the role of the host. Let the rules of social order and compliance that we have all been taught work in your favour. The key is to proactively take the lead before you actually need to exercise leadership. It is vital to point out that setting the scene should not be understood as a manipulation attempt. A high-stakes negotiation causes stress levels to rise. When stakes are high, so are emotions. Therefore, **the more uncomfortable it is on the inside, the more agreeable it should be on the outside**. You must never forget about creating a relationship of trust and engaging the other party in a genuine, sincere and honest manner. Below is a tool that will help you set the right tone.

Negotiation host checklist

- The shape of the table can have an impact on the negotiation. Especially when many people are involved, very long tables make it difficult for people to see anyone on the opposite end. This can create a feeling of alienation. Strive for a sense of inclusion.

- Choose the seating arrangement wisely. It is you who should place the name cards and direct people to their seats. Otherwise, all the representatives of party A will naturally sit on one side of the table, while all the representatives of party B will take their seats on the opposite side.

- Make sure no mistakes are made on the name cards. Double-check the spelling of names and the proper titles.

- Decide what equipment you will need. Work materials such as projectors, pens and notepads should be available; the presentation (if applicable) should be well organised; and everything should be tested so that technical issues are avoided.

- Make sure there is a whiteboard or a flipchart at your disposal. This is a very powerful tool of persuasion. You can write your demands down on the board or flipchart and have them in full sight all through the meeting. The longer your negotiation partner looks at your demands, the more they subconsciously embrace them. Soon enough your demands will become a part of their reality.

- Consider how many copies of documents you make available. Beware that if everyone has their 'own' copy, even if it's the same document, the ownership effect will kick in. The same document will then become *your* and *their* version. It might be better to open a share screen option and have everyone contribute while one person (you or a member of your team) writes down the points under discussion and what was agreed on.

- Do not order catering. Go out for coffee/tea or lunch instead. Leaving the meeting room liberates the mind. It is like going on the symbolic emotional

▶

balcony where you distance yourself from the action, except that you physically move. The symbolic act of walking together in one direction has a powerful effect. It is worth noting that you cannot walk face-to-face, only shoulder to shoulder – in a collaborative rather than a confrontational manner.

- Have refreshments available. Not offering any is perceived as rude and condescending. Healthy snacks such as nuts or fruits are better than energy drinks that artificially pump the negotiators up.

- Pay attention to the ambience of the negotiation room: comfortable chairs, adequate light (not too bright, not too low), pleasant temperature, fresh flowers and small gifts or courtesies set the mood for cooperation.

Summary of key take-aways

1 Align strategic preparation with a positive attitude.

2 Create the three grand negotiation illusions: autonomy and choice, ownership and victory.

3 In a high-stakes negotiation, the more uncomfortable it is on the inside, the more agreeable you should make it on the outside.

4 Be the host both for the process, for yourself and for the other party.

5 Create a relationship of trust and engage the other party in a genuine, sincere and honest manner.

Further reading

1 Lempereur, A. and Colson, A. (2010) *The First Move: A Negotiator's Companion.* John Wiley & Sons.

2 Opresnik, M.O. (2014) *The Hidden Rules of Successful Negotiation and Communication' 13: Management for Professionals.* Switzerland: Springer International Publishing.

3 PON staff (2016) In Business Negotiations, Set the Stage for Success: Through intensive planning, the organizers of the Paris climate-change talks streamlined a massively complex negotiation. 12 February 2016.

4 Shonk, K. (2019) *Online Negotiation Strategies: Email and Videoconferencing.* Harvard Law School.

CHAPTER 9
CREATING VALUE IN NEGOTIATIONS

'Compound interest is the eighth wonder of the world. He who understands it, earns it . . . he who doesn't . . . pays it.'

Unattributed

What you will discover in this chapter:

- How to add value to high-stakes negotiations
- Common challenges related to creating value and how to overcome them
- What are the three pillars of value-focused negotiation?
- The conditions for creating value

Why is it important to create value in negotiations?

In today's business environment, value adding has become the standard. Value creating is the premium. The condition for value-oriented negotiations is a switch from the I-focus. The selfie culture, characterised by an obsession with oneself, has spread from social media to human interactions. This trend is also visible in the professional sphere. One of the participants in my training recently said that when he listens to his business partners and clients, the words that stand out the most are 'me, myself, and I'.

This orientation is particularly visible in job negotiations. Seldom do I see a cover letter that highlights the value that the candidate will bring to the firm.

The majority of applicants describe what they want to get out of working for the company (I want to work for/learn from the best, I want to thrive with you, I want to build a career, and so on). This is an environment filled with opportunities. Negotiators who can expand their vision beyond the self-centred limits can gain a strong competitive advantage. In this chapter you will discover how to align perceived value with your negotiation approach. We will start with a deep dive into one of the frequently encountered business situations.

Value-focused negotiations

Imagine the following scenario. You are a consultant providing training services to large multinational companies. You receive a request for proposal (RFP) from one of your prospects. They need your assistance with setting up a negotiation strategy for the upcoming discussions with their business partner. If the talks go successfully for them, they will expand their geographic scope and enter into a new partnership. Due to the high stakes of the deal, they need a professional negotiation approach. You send them your proposal, the receipt of which they immediately confirm with a simple thank you message. Then follows a period of silence. After two weeks you decide to follow up on your communication. As a result, you are invited to a face-to-face meeting with the managing director in charge of the project. They are to be your main contact person.

Due to the complexity of the deal that you are to help them with, your offering includes many points that need to be discussed, such as confidentiality clauses, scope of assistance, consulting rates, length of support, delivery terms, responsibilities, and so on. The talks with your direct contact, the managing director, take several weeks. After about two months you get an invitation to meet with the head of procurement. You set up another in-person meeting. When you arrive to their office, you meet the head of procurement. Her behaviour towards you is reserved and she seems unimpressed with the progress of the ongoing talks and your offering.

She opens the meeting by saying that it is an extremely busy time for the company and that she only has 20 minutes for you. She suggests getting straight to the point. 'If you do not give us a 25 per cent discount on your initial proposal, then we do not have a deal', she throws your way and expectantly looks at you in silence.

Your task: Before you read on, take a moment to reflect what you feel and how you would react. First, write down all your initial thoughts as they come. Then, draft up a response plan. When you are done, take a moment to reflect both on your initial reflections and the logic of your plan. Now answer the following questions.

Questions for you:

Do you really think that the prospect is interested in closing the deal with you? Yes/No?

Which elements of the scenario did you focus on the most?

Does your response plan include value creation?

The fundamental question is whether your prospect is serious about closing the deal with you. This realisation will be the driving force of your reaction, and it will also impact whether you focus on counter-offering or value creating. To answer this, we must look below the surface of what is happening. This case is packed with tactics outlined below.

- Silence following the initial receipt of your proposal.
- Several weeks of talks that translate into time investment drawing you deeper into the process and thus making you less willing to waste the time by losing the potential deal.
- Switch of negotiation partner – anytime a new player enters the scene, the energy and dynamic will change.
- Bringing in the head of procurement for effect. Due to the role, the expectancy will be a focus on financials, which is indeed the demand she makes.
- Reserved and unimpressed behaviour of the head of procurement:
  - Yet again, the point is to make you doubt the attractiveness of your proposal.
  - Some negotiators would also try to 'warm up' the behaviour, which would derail their focus from the main objective of the meeting.
- The head of procurement calling the shots by opening and stating the terms.
- Time pressure and a 20-minute deadline.
- A big demand of a 25 per cent price slash served in the form of a threat (*if you do not do this, then this will happen*).

Judging by the amount of tactics, there is a strong interest in finding an agreement with you. Whenever you have the impression that the reaction of the other party is exaggerated tactically, then you can be pretty much sure that you are in for a close. The natural impulse that many professionals have in this type of situation is to counter-offer. They focus their attention on presenting arguments to justify the 'fairness' of their proposal, they get anxious when presented with a deadline in fear of losing the deal and consequently they risk committing to less-than-favourable terms. Most importantly, their energy is channelled to price discussions, whereas the focus should be on value. In order to avoid a zero-sum discussion, it is worth investing time to understand the value perception of your negotiation partner. Specifically, look beyond the borders of the negotiation with you. The other party has stakeholders whose interests they want to satisfy through the deal with you. This is where the real value of the negotiation with you lies.

Common challenges related to creating value

Based on my exchanges with business professionals, I have identified the three most common challenges that relate to creating value in high-stakes negotiations. They are as follows:

Challenge #1: How can I explain the value of my offer to the other party?
How to overcome it:

Value, like beauty, is in the eye of the beholder. You cannot justify a subjective perspective to someone who may not share the same paradigm as you. Instead of explaining why your deal is valuable, focus on understanding what is desirable for *them*. How do they define value? Once you comprehend their value system, you can dress up your proposal to appeal to their tastes.

Challenge #2: How can I change the focus from price driven to value?
How to overcome it:

The iceberg theory discussed in Chapter 12 will be helpful. Identify what the price (their position = tip of the iceberg) represents. Uncover what interests, motives and needs are driving that position (what is below the water). What you are basically doing is trying to comprehend their *perception* of value. Once you have done this, align the perceived value with the pricing discussion. You may also expand the scope of the deal so that the value field is broader and then steer the conversation towards the financials. If they do not care about the value at all and pricing is all that matters, then you need to consider whether the deal adds value for you. No-deal is a legitimate option. We will discuss this topic in more detail in Chapter 13, which is dedicated to closing the negotiation.

Challenge #3: How do I bridge the need to spend enough time on value realisation versus closing the deal?
How to overcome it:

By rushing to close the deal you may miss out on opportunities to add future value for both parties. Value-focused negotiations take more time and effort; however, they make the end result more. . . valuable. It may happen that the other party does not fully understand what exactly they need. This is often the case when clients reach out to consulting or training firms. They see the symptoms of an organisational problem, but without fully getting to the roots of what is causing it. Your task will be to identify the causes that will shape your value proposition and only then to present the benefits of the proposal you are making them.

The three pillars of value-focused negotiations

Creating value works on three levels:

1   The deal (the task that both negotiators set out to achieve),
2   The relationship between the parties,
3   External value.

Bringing value to the deal – the ZOPA and ZON

The first element is fairly easy to manage, because it is based on the financial assessment of the negotiation. From a monetary perspective, you can use two benchmarks to judge whether a deal makes sense. The first one is the Zone of Possible Agreement (ZOPA). This concept measures whether there is a financial overlap between the expectations of both parties. In a sales transaction this would be the maximum that the buyer is willing to pay and the minimum that the seller is willing to accept for the good. If the deal lies within the ZOPA of both negotiators, then it brings monetary value to both of them.

The second is the designated by your Zone of Negotiation (ZON) – the zone depicted by the maximum (aspirational) and minimum target that you have established for a particular negotiation. Provided that you stay with your ZON, the deal has monetary value for you.

Creating value in the relationship – the two reserves

Unless the negotiation is a one-off event, the assessment of the deal goes beyond pure task orientation. A long-lasting and executable agreement is one where the objectives are reached, and the relationship between the parties is strengthened. Business is personal; people want to deal with partners whom they can trust and rely on. It may happen that you will not be able to meet all the financial requirements of the other party, but your negotiation style and approach will be equally valuable for them. You can inject value to the deal by investing in the relationship.

A simple tool is the two reserves. At the start of the negotiation imagine that you are opening two accounts, a positive and a negative reserve. The latter one represents the challenges or obstacles that you will inevitably face on your path to agreement. The positive account is the one that you should invest in on a daily basis, so that when the rainy day comes, you can offset the negative with the positives. Figure 9.1 lists some examples of what you can fuel the accounts with. As you will notice, the trick is for the positives to outweigh the negatives.

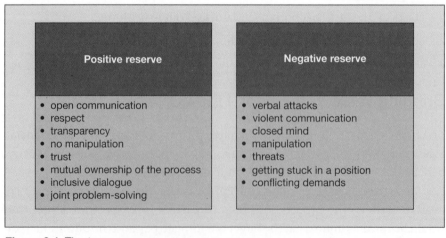

Figure 9.1 The two reserves

External value – the Y–T–S system

The last pillar of value creating is not the typical element that negotiators think about. If you look at the three main challenges that were discussed earlier, you will notice that value propositions are usually limited to the sphere of the deal between the two parties. This dual outlook omits one important element – the external environment and more specifically, the stakeholders.

A negotiation outcome is broader than the deal itself. It has external implications for both parties. In order to create value, you need to consider the consequences of the deal for the other party – all the circumstances that lay outside the framework of their negotiation with you. Let us take the example of a company offering IT solutions to its clients. When the IT firm negotiates with their customer, the best way for them to convince them is by showing the value of the negotiated products and services not directly related to them, but rather to *their* clients and stakeholders (the third party to the IT firm).

This is what I refer to as the Y–T–S (You–Them–Stakeholders) system as illustrated in Figure 9.2. Practical application tip: Look for the external value outside of the direct scope of your negotiation with the other party.

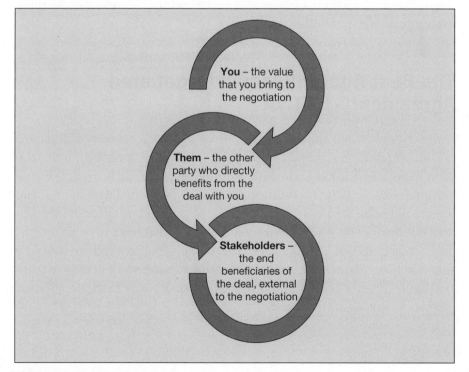

Figure 9.2 The Y–T–S system

The conditions for creating value

The ability to induce value is one of the essential skills of a successful negotiator. Therefore, it is necessary to understand what the prerequisites of value-focused negotiations are. Value creation is considered to be a strategic, process-oriented undertaking. Nonetheless, it requires that the negotiator enjoys a certain psychological setting. Value-driven negotiating requires the ability to look beyond the position (demands) of the other party (what we referred to before as the tip of the iceberg). Only when this is achieved can creativity flow. It is also recommended to intellectually go off the beaten track. Looking for inspiration beyond your playing field and your industry is a great way to boost the creative process.

Contrary to artists who conceive some of their best works under the influence of strong emotions, creativity in negotiations necessitates a rational approach combined with a quiet and relaxed mind. Such a state is only possible when you have alternatives. There is nothing worse for innovation than the feeling that you have a knife at your throat in a negotiation.

We will now look in more detail at the two popular concepts of BATNA (Best Alternative to Negotiated Agreement) and options and how you can use them to create value in your deal-making.

The Best Alternative to a Negotiated Agreement – BATNA

Power in negotiations flows from the perception that a negotiator has access to multiple resources that their opponent does not. The simple logic is that the party with access to more resources is more independent and less reliant on the outcome of the deal. BATNA is the ultimate tool of internal liberation. If you want to add value, start by securing multiple alternatives *outside* of the negotiation. Psychologically, your BATNA is a condition for the ability to create options (more on options later). The more external options you have and can convince your negotiator partner that you have, the more valuable you will seem to them as a partner. They will be more motivated to also add value to the deal, so that you choose to close with them.

Conventional approaches to deal-making usually focus on generating and evaluating alternatives; however, they fail to point out that alternatives are only tools to achieve value. Another limiting factor is that the range of alternatives that negotiators identify for a given decision is often too narrow. As an example, when applying for a job one will typically only compare a job offer to the current job and will not create other alternatives, such as a job in another city or country. Therefore, the most creative or different alternatives remain hidden.

Here are the three steps to creating the best alternatives:

1 Focus on one objective at a time.

2 Then combine the objectives and re-evaluate them.

3 Consider the strategic objective that is the widest one.

Creating and framing options

There is a difference between BATNA and options. Options are all the things that both parties can agree on within a given negotiation, and anything that can happen *inside* that negotiation. Alternatives refer to possibilities *outside* of the negotiation – the solutions you have *outside* of the current negotiation (should you decide not to close the deal), and the outcomes you can reach on your own, without obtaining the agreement of your counterpart.

Before you create options, you need to consider how to frame the deal. The concept of framing in negotiations refers to the fact that the way we formulate our offer strongly affects how our counterpart views it.

There are three strategies that can help you successfully frame options.

1 **Offer three choices:** Studies on marketing and consumer behaviour suggest that people prefer fewer rather than more choices, which is a pertinent finding for framing in negotiation. When proposing too many options a party can become overwhelmed and prefer not to choose at all. Therefore, limiting the options that you propose is advised. Do not offer more than three options.

2 **Make several offers:** Although it is important to limit choices, research suggests that issuing three equivalent offers can be a good strategy. When you present multiple offers you grant the liberty of choice to the other party and their reactions will tell you about their priorities.

3   **Plan rejection:** The contrast concept proposes the idea that an offer will
    seem more attractive when compared to another lower one. This effect
    suggests a strategic psychological move for negotiations. Ask for more than
    you actually want and expect rejection before you reduce your offer. The
    second offer is likely to seem a lot more appealing after the rejection.

Creativity in negotiations

Creativity is a helpful tool to transform negotiations from distributive (splitting
the pie) to integrative (baking a larger one). As an example, a car seller could
bring a guarantee certificate which might make it easier for the buyer to make
concessions related to the price.

There are several ways in which you can introduce value using creativity.

- **Logrolling:** The concept of logrolling refers to the exchange of concessions
  on low- versus high-value issues. Logrolling aims for better mutual outcomes
  rather than compromises. Therefore, both parties can make concessions on
  the issues that are less valuable to them and achieve a better joint outcome.
  Many negotiators miss the chance to logroll because of the fixed-pie perception. In order to make the best package deals, negotiators must overcome
  this perception and understand that negotiators value the discussed issues
  differently.

- **Exploiting compatible interests:** Usually when entering a business deal,
  you and your counterpart will have compatible interests and preferences
  within these issues. By exchanging sufficient information, the two parties
  stand a better chance of realising the full potential of these commonalities
  and therefore finding a mutually satisfying agreement.

- **Expanding the resource:** The common instinct is to immediately jump
  into zero-sum price discussions, which result in compromise or one-sided
  concessions. Instead, it is recommended to add additional scope to the deal
  and only then to make concessions.

- **Unbundling issues:** When closely inspecting any negotiation, negotiators
  often discover that there are many issues other than price. When unbundling issues, the newly emerged negotiation agenda can contain valuable
  information for logrolling or for exploiting compatible interests.

- **Contingent contract:** A contract in which both parties agree on a lower selling price and additional future payments which are contingent on future earnings. This is a creative solution for both parties with the added value of risk sharing.

Expert view

Lieutenant Jack Cambria
Instructor, Police Advisor, Corporate Trainer, NYPD Hostage Team Commander, New York, USA

Although the principles of corporate and police negotiations are almost identical, the two situations cannot compare in terms of the level of challenges related to crafting alternative courses of action. In the business setting, you have the ability to plan in advance before you meet the other party. This allows you to research all the issues and to get to know the negotiator on the other side. You can agree on a mutual time and place, set up a luncheon or reconvene the next day if you find you may need a break or a recess to re-visit the issue.

A crisis negotiator does not have all these luxuries. They get the assignment and need to start with developing the strategy without setting the scene. It's a little like walking into a cinema in the middle of a movie, when the action is already in the middle-act. You then need to back-track the investigation to establish what happened and build rapport with hostile individuals, such as convicts, people who are no longer in control of themselves, and suicide attempts. Dealing with difficult negotiation partners takes time.

To overcome some of these challenges, it is recommended to have the element of tactical presence in place. For example, at the NYPD we often used what we called a motivator. If the hostage taker did not want to talk to us (NYPD negotiators), we would introduce tactical presence in the form of the SWAT team. The hostage taker could look out the window and see the building surrounded by the SWAT team with their weapons. The alternative would be talking to us. Once you establish a line of communication, you need to engage in active listening. Your objective is to find a hook and use it as a motivating factor to impact the behaviour. A hook can be anything, a child, a pet, a family that is waiting at home with dinner. You use this information about the other party to show them what would be the consequences of escalation, for example loss of custody over the child, the pet being taken to a shelter, the rejection by family members in the case of arrest, and so on. By showing the downsides of the escalation path, you can motivate the other party to start cooperating with you.

Summary of key take-aways

1 Value adding is the standard; value creating is the premium.

2 Creating value in negotiations starts by changing the I-focus.

3 A long-lasting and valuable agreement is one where the objectives are reached, and the relationship between the parties is strengthened. Make sure you invest in the relation.

4 Look for the external value outside of the direct scope of your negotiation with the other party.

5 You increase your value to the other party when you make them believe that you have alternatives and can create interesting options for them.

Further reading

1 Giebels, E., Dreu, C.K.W. and Van de Vliert, E. (2000) Interdependence in negotiation: effects of exit options and social motives on distributive and integrative negotiation. *European Journal of Social Psychology* 30, 255–272.

2 Hüffmeier, J. and Hertel, G. (2014) Creativity in negotiations. *Negotiation Excellence*, pp. 59–77.

3 Keeney, R.L. (1994) Creativity in decision making with value-focused thinking. *Sloan Management Review*.

4 Putnam, L.L. (2010) Communication as changing the negotiation game. *Journal of Applied Communication Research* 38 (4), 325–335.

5 Shonk, K. (2021) Framing in negotiation. Program on Negotiation, Harvard Law School, Daily Blog.

6 Shonk, K. (2021) Principled negotiation: focus on interests to create value. 1 February 2021. Program on Negotiation, Harvard Law School, Daily Blog.

7 Vidar, S. (2013) Creative people create values: creativity and positive arousal in negotiations. *Creativity Research Journal* 25 (4), 408–417, DOI: 10.1080/10400419.2013.843336

CHAPTER 10
TAKING THE LEAD IN THE NEGOTIATION

'A leader is one who knows the way, goes the way, and shows the way.'

John Maxwell

What you will discover in this chapter:

- The distinction between power and authority and how to establish both
- What are the traits of a leader-negotiator
- Deciding the specific roles and who does what in the negotiation

Why how you lead a negotiation is important

Negotiation is a balancing act between people and process management. Leading the human factor is a prerequisite for the success of the deal. In order to successfully conclude the negotiation, two things need to occur: the negotiated terms should be executable and a business bond between the parties should be established and reinforced. Consequently, the negotiator needs to be a good strategist who is able to navigate the interpersonal dynamics, specifically by understanding what makes people want to follow. We will now explore how to approach both challenges with relational finesse mixed with business savvy.

The difference between power and authority

As we already discovered, power on the external level is the capacity to get the other person to do what they would not have done without our intervention. The problem with that approach is grasped by the saying 'He who complies against his will, is of his opinion still' (S. Butler). Agreement without a buy-in has a short shelf life. A forced agreement is worse than no agreement, because it will neither fulfil the task in the long run, nor will it strengthen the relationship between the parties. The condition for an executable agreement is therefore getting the other side to comply with your asks out of their free will. In order for that to happen, you need to have authority. Authority is influence that is based on perceived legitimacy. The key word is *perceived*. For people to want to follow, they need to see and accept you as a credible (authority) figure. The differentiation between power and authority is visible in the definitions of management and leadership.

Management is the process of directing, coordinating, controlling and planning the work of others. The focus is primarily process- or task-oriented. Leadership relates to developing ideas and a vision, living by values that support those ideas and that vision, and influencing others to embrace them in their own behaviours. A manager can be appointed and equipped with power, but that does not necessarily make them a leader in the eyes of the other party. In order to become the latter, it is always more important to understand the other party first – what are their beliefs, their values and their vision? Only when they feel that these resonate with your own can wilful compliance be made possible. Leadership combines the relational aspect with the task factor. The focus of this chapter will be to distinguish between management and leadership in relation to the allocation of negotiation roles.

The typical mistake that unskilled negotiators make is that they try to exert power and pressure. The paradox of power lies in its subtlety. Those who feel powerful do not need to prove that they are, neither to themselves nor to the other party. Dominance can be exercised by verbal or physical overpowering, such as for example a knuckle-whitening handshake. Ironically, the most dangerous negotiator is often the nicest and the seemingly least powerful one.

Agatha Christie, the British queen of crime fiction, created two distinctive detective protagonists, the famous Hercule Poirot and the less known Miss

Marple. The latter was an old spinster from a little English village called St. Mary Mead. The success record of Miss Marple was impressive, although she was the less spectacular of the two protagonists. Her method relied on the observation of the universal laws of human nature. The little town where she lived served as a nutshell of the typology of human characters. Miss Marple's mastery of profiling allowed her to solve many murders and other crimes. Her tactic was simple: play naïve (aka dumb), harmless and clueless to the external eye. Because she projected somewhat limited power, people often let their guard down around her. Hercule Poirot often announced himself to be 'the greatest detective of all times'. This caused caution, reservation and sometimes led to a power struggle for first place on the alpha podium. Miss Marple's methods were humbler yet equally successful in the final outcome.

Here is an example of how you can use the Miss Marple limited power approach in your negotiations:

> **I heard what you said and will pass the information on to my boss. I think this will be a challenging issue for us, however we will take a serious look at what you are proposing. While I have been chosen to lead the discussions with you, I am not the final decision maker. I will get back to you on this.**

You may or may not be the final decision maker. The benefit for you is that you win time and do not commit too early. By downplaying your power, you make the other side less cautious around you. From my own experience, the worse deals I ever made were when I admitted that I am a negotiation consultant. The result of that confession was usually a 15 per cent increase of the counter-offer and an attempt of the other party to prove their negotiation prowess to me. Admitting your power, which can often be accentuated when you feel you do not have full control, is a strong stimulant for a counter show of force. It is recommended to rely on authority rather than on power alone.

How to establish your power?

Insights from practice indicate that power is related to the ability of building a relationship of trust while also managing the process. It therefore requires the mastery of soft and hard skills.

Expert view

Benita Hess
Director Life Sciences at KPMG, Switzerland

To start, we need to determine what we understand by power in high-stakes negotiations. There are two crucial conditions of a successful negotiation – a secure environment and a shared mindset governed by mutual respect between the parties. Great negotiations can only happen with equal trust and a similar level of power. An imbalance of power (real or perceived) will close up the other party to compromise.

Power in negotiations is therefore enhanced by a solid foundation – in the form of a robust relationship. If you want a sustainable cooperation, you need to be ready to invest time and commitment towards the other. The agreement you reach cannot be single-sided. In high-stakes negotiations you need to have a clear strategy and know what your objective is. Be well prepared. You should have a concrete understanding of where you want to end up before you start negotiating. You also need to be willing to compromise. Don't underestimate that a lot of pre-work is necessary, both on the tactical and interpersonal level.

There are several factors that are necessary for reaching an executable agreement. The requirements are a combination of hard and soft skills. They are as follows:

● The tactical prowess for reaching your negotiation objective is one of the hard skills you need to acquire (and own).

● Soft skills (can be trained) – effective communication skills, the ability to listen, problem-solving skills, decision-making skills, the ability to deal with different people and situations and the ability to reduce misunderstandings.

To sum up, the array of skills, the ability to compromise, collaborate and accommodate, along with trust and respect, are key to unlock the negotiation power in high-stakes deals. Be clear in what you want to say and achieve and have enough perseverance to stick to it.

The negotiator as a leader

Leadership is more than just a position or a place on an organisation chart; it reflects a role as well as a set of functions and corresponding behaviours. Looking at the big picture, leadership can be regarded as the change of a relationship, as well as a resource allocation to negotiating large organisational changes. This resembles the task and relationship elements of the negotiation process. It also points to the fact that the disciplines of negotiation and leadership are related. The behavioural attributes which are necessary for effective negotiators complement certain leadership traits. Together they form the leader-negotiator ecosystem.

- **The negotiator as a secure base.** The substantive issues, such as the logic, assumptions, ideological beliefs and emotional patterns of the leader can reinforce their reasoning and intuitive perceptions. These factors can then heavily impact the negotiation by winning followers. The condition for that to happen is that the assumptions of the leader-negotiator mirror those of the other party. A secure base negotiator is in control of their mindset, the people and the process, as shown in Figure 10.1.

- **Managing the mindset.** Similar to negotiation, leadership starts from within. Therefore, the most difficult negotiations to conduct are with the personal suppositions that could sabotage the negotiation. Typical mind defaults that could jeopardise the chances for success are based on assumptions that:
  - the past and the future must be related;
  - avoiding or oversimplifying complex issues is an advantage;
  - all problems and parties can be approached in the same way;
  - there exist one-size-fits-all solutions.

- **Managing the people.** Success depends on the openness to new ideas and the effort to understand the others' values in a joint attempt to improve the negotiated outcome. Leaders who are blinded by bias, operate according to stereotypes, have difficulty in embracing diversity or fall prey to their own habitual patterns of behaviour may limit the chances for cooperation.

- **Managing the process.** Negotiations consist of four sequences: before, beginning, during and closing. Different tactics must be used to lead through the different sequences of the negotiation. In the preparation phase it is important to gather the important information. In the beginning of the negotiation it is recommended to mostly observe and listen. Moving further in the negotiation requires a certain level of assertiveness in introducing demands and making concessions that can lead to a successful outcome. Towards the end it is appropriate to give alternatives to close and seal the deal.

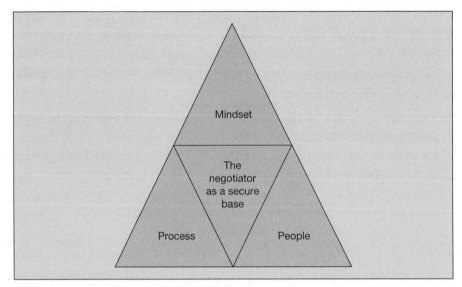

Figure 10.1 The leader-negotiator ecosystem

A leader-negotiator needs to feel at ease in all these aspects. The concept of a leader-negotiator is not to be confused with a lead negotiator, which is a strategic role. A leader-negotiator is someone who displays a leadership mindset and possesses corresponding traits that are compelling to followers.

Which style to choose?

A negotiator in charge of the process can choose between three leadership styles.

1 Coercive

2 Normative

3 Utilitarian

Coercive approach

The coercive approach relies on persuasion by the use of power, either in the form of reward or punishment. Taking something away, for example placing a time limit on an offer, taking away a loyalty discount or preferred supplier status, can be a strong stimulant for the other party.

When to use the coercive approach: When the other party is stubbornly in an uncooperative mood, does not acknowledge your status or when it is a one-off deal.

Normative approach

The normative approach is an appeal to a person's values and beliefs. It is often exercised by creating cognitive dissonance, a state of the mind in which evidence (objective or fabricated by the other party) conflicts with a person's worldview, values and beliefs. It works in the following manner. If you want to ask a person to agree to a big cause, start by securing commitment to a chunk of your final aspirational goal. For example, if you are seeking donation for the preservation of wildlife species, have them agree to putting a sticker with the cause on their premises. Let the identity of a wildlife species activist set in. Then come back with the big demand. Once they see themselves as a supporter, it will be more difficult for them to reject your request.

When to use the normative approach: With highly opinionated people who have a strong need for autonomy and only after you have understood what their values and beliefs are.

Note of caution: To be used only for a good cause. It is justifiable for the other party to reject the normative approach if you are working in bad faith.

Utilitarian approach

The utilitarian approach appeals to a person's self-interest or implication of possible benefits. It answers the basic question: What's in it for me? Negotiation is not philanthropy. It is a game of trade and you are both in it to satisfy your interests; otherwise there would not be a discussion.

When to use the utilitarian approach: Practically at all times. You need to show your negotiation partner why the deal is beneficial for them. This is the condition for securing their buy in and long-lasting commitment to the negotiated terms.

Expert view

Alessandro Soldati
CEO at Goldavenue, Switzerland

The leadership approach depends on the type of negotiation. In high-stakes negotiations, for example in the precious metal industry, it is important to know who the decision-makers are. If you are talking to a lawyer, who is acting as an intermediary between you and the customer (the real decision-maker), you need to be careful how you structure the information flow and information sharing. You need to ensure that what you said will not be distorted when it reaches the ears of the final decision-maker. Another factor relates to information asymmetry. The negotiator who is leading the discussion needs to know how much information the other party has. Do they already have an idea of the best price, how educated are they about the specifics of the industry, and how knowledgeable are they about this type of transaction? The more information you equip yourself with, the better you can lead the negotiation. Information is power in the sense that it will allow you to lead the negotiation from a position of confidence.

It is important to know how many competitors are in the arena in a high-stakes deal. For example, you need to be careful that your customer does not use the information you provide to get a better deal with your competitor. You need to balance how much you share. This is not easy, because you need to say enough for them to be able to make their decision, but not overshare. Always let the other party do more of the talking. Get information before you give information. Lead by listening.

Deciding the strategic roles

A prevailing misconception is that negotiation is a one-man show. This is certainly not the case in High-Impact negotiations. One person cannot be the conductor and the orchestra. For an effective process, it is recommended to set up a negotiation team that consists of three roles:

- the master mind (MM) – the decision maker;
- the master of ceremony (MC) – the negotiator;
- and the mentor negotiator (MN).

The responsibilities and silhouette of each persona as well as the interplay of these roles are discussed below.

The master mind (MM) responsibilities

Strategic set-up – planning, directing and controlling the negotiation. This involves:

- defining the mission statement;
- establishing the goal and objective, including maximum and minimum target;

- deciding on the timeframe for the negotiation;
- organising the team roles;
- making the final decision.

Someone who is fit for the MM role needs to have the following traits:

- ability to think strategically and have a long-term vision;
- no tendency for micromanagement (so that they do not take over the MC role);
- no usurpation of power;
- good planning skills;
- proper judge of character to appoint the MC and MN;
- high degree of responsibility and accountability;
- ability to make decisions and stick to them.

The master of ceremony (MC) responsibilities

Strategic execution and leadership – developing an idea and a vision, embodying values that support that idea and vision, and convincing the other party to follow. This involves:

- focusing on the task part;
- gathering the necessary information;
- deciding on the right strategy and implementing it;
- presenting demands;
- creating value;
- closing the deal.

Someone who is fit for the MC role needs to have the following traits:

- strong self-management skills;
- effective communication skills;
- ability to see the details;
- immunity to stress and pressure;
- a good balance between power and authority;
- charisma and stage presence;
- assertiveness;

- good problem-solving skills;
- a tough heart: knowing when to replace people who don't succeed.

The mentor negotiator (MN) responsibilities

A stabilising agent for the MC and an interface between the MM and the MC. This involves:

- serving as the eyes and ears of the negotiation;
- the ability to see the big picture and things that the MC might miss in the heat of the action;
- being an objective, silent observer;
- understanding the underlying needs and motivation of the other party;
- creating a positive atmosphere by focusing more on the relationship than the task.

Someone who is fit for the MN role needs to have the following traits:

- strong level of self-control (so that they do not get pulled in the discussion and lose their objectivity);
- good judge of character;
- excellent observation skills;
- an authority figure for the negotiator;
- an appeasing presence;
- ability to see the big picture.

How these roles work together

The process starts with the MC who introduces the negotiation strategy (mission statement, goal and objective) and designates the strategic team roles. The MN serves as a link between the MM and the MC, and as a stabilising factor for the MC. The MC is responsible for leading the interaction with the other party and for strategic execution (gathering information, choice of strategy, dealing, creating value and closing). The MM makes the final decision. The interplay of the three roles is presented in Figure 10.2.

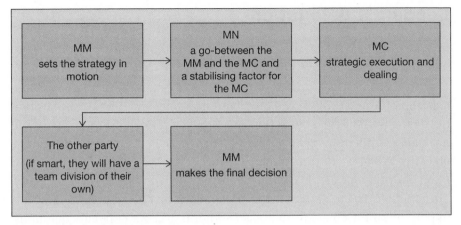

Figure 10.2 The interplay of roles

The more the merrier?

Practitioners often wonder whether strength lies in the numbers. If the other party brings several people to the discussion, should you double your head count? Apart from impression management, there are more risks than benefits from allowing too many participants. The dangers of large negotiation teams are groupthink, loss of individual responsibility, suggestibility and lack of consensus. For those reasons I recommend a lean organigram made up of the three roles of MM, MC and MN.

You can control the process at your end. Should you find yourself in a negotiation with multiple parties, here are specific techniques you can use.

- Lay down ground rules for the negotiation.
- 100 per cent consensus is a myth. Forget about trying to satisfy everybody.
- Control the negotiation process and don't allow one person to hijack it. For example, if one party refuses to budge, it is better to focus on those parties that risk being swayed by the one who is trying to block the deal. This can build a strong coalition and make the deal-blocker choose between getting on board with the deal or being left behind.
- In order to control large groups, it is better to break them down to manageable sizes.
- The same goes for large issues; break them down into smaller issues that will be discussed.

Leading a delegation

In order to manage a delegation of negotiators and lead them properly, the master mind can designate a chief master of ceremony – the negotiator in charge of the delegation. The MC must be well prepared, assess the team (the psychological profile and skillset) and distribute clear roles and lines of responsibilities. Power must be clear but at the same time the group must be on board and not want to undermine their authority. There must be a constant focus on the objective as well as alignment on the process. All the team members should be on one page and should communicate the same message to the other party. The chief MC has to designate a clear approach for the group to follow. It is important for the chief MC to not act authoritative, but rather ask questions, build an environment of trust and inclusive dialogue, and lead in a democratic manner. Finally, they should be held accountable for the decisions that they make.

Summary of key take-aways

1 Negotiation is a combination of management and leadership skills.

2 Projecting somewhat limited power (the Miss Marple approach) is more useful than engaging in a power struggle.

3 Exercising power without building a robust relationship will not lead to an executable agreement.

4 A great negotiator-leader is someone who the other party wants to willingly follow.

5 Deciding on the roles involves strategic planning and finding a psychological fit.

Further reading

1 Hiebert, M. and Klatt, B. (2001) *The Encyclopedia of Leadership – A Practical Guide to Popular Leadership Theories and Techniques.* McGraw-Hill.

2 Kray, L.J. (2007) Leading through negotiation: harnessing the power of gender stereotypes. *California Management Review* 50 (1).

3   Long, B.S. (2016) Collective bargaining as the negotiation of competing stories: Implications for leadership. *Journal of Strategic Contracting and Negotiation* 2 (1–2).

4   Pon Staff (2020) Techniques for Leading Multiparty Negotiations: Structuring the Bargaining Process, Negotiation techniques from great negotiator Tommy Koh on how to lead multiparty negotiations. Pon Staff, November 2020.

5   Salacuse, J.W. (2017) *Real Leaders Negotiate – Gaining, Using and Keeping the Power to Lead Through Negotiation.* The Fletcher School of Law and Diplomacy, Tufts University, Medford, Massachusetts, 6 January 2017.

6   Saner, R. (2012) *The Expert Negotiator.* Leiden/Boston: Martinus Nijhoff Publishers.

7   Sylvester, K. (2016) *Negotiating in the Leadership Zone.* Colorado Springs: Elsevier Inc.

8   Zohar, I. (2015) *The Art of Negotiation – Leadership Skills Required for Negotiation in Time of Crisis.* Bolyai University Cluj-Napoca, Romania.

CHAPTER 11
OPENING THE
NEGOTIATION

'Start out with an ideal and end up with a deal.'

Karl Albrecht

What you will discover in this chapter:

- Things to take into account when opening a negotiation
- What the anchoring effect is and how to manage it
- How to design a successful agenda

Opening a negotiation

Even experienced negotiators can feel stressed and uneasy about beginning a new negotiation. When we prepare for a negotiation, we usually have the luxury of being in a controlled environment, in a place and at a time of our choice. The opening phase is far less predictable and safe, because it is the moment when two parties come together. It is no longer as easy to predict how the dynamic will unfold. This causes stress levels to rise. The impact of these anxious feelings does not have to be entirely negative. If managed well, they can spark creativity in terms of the task and help support a constructive relationship.

Openings are affected by performance anxiety, first impressions and uncertainty. These factors should be carefully considered before entering the negotiation.

- **Performance anxiety.** The thought of performing can cause anxiety, especially for high-stakes negotiations where a lot of pressure is involved. The importance attributed to the nature of the negotiation can inflict self-doubt. It can become a self-fulfilling prophecy. The more anxious you are, the more the other party will pick up on the nervousness and take it as a sign of weakness. Negotiators who struggle with self-doubt and lack of conviction come across as less credible and are less effective in the strategic and tactical execution. This is why opening requires a fine balance between a solid preparation (a proactive approach) – the elements that were discussed in Part I – and being able to react to elements of surprise.

- **Getting off on the wrong foot.** First impressions are formed in a matter of seconds and are very hard to change. Our brains have been wired to operate in shortcuts. This is due to a combination of primal instincts and our personal experiences through which we quickly determine the difference between 'friend or foe'. Openings are the moment when anticipation meets reality and when we test the accuracy of the information we have gathered during preparation.

- **Uncertainty.** Openings come with great momentum, because on one hand they require commitment to our goal, but on the other the realisation of that goal will partially depend on the other party whose reactions are unpredictable. A big mistake in negotiations is starting from a self-centred perspective, which is often perceived as judgemental and provocative. This approach can then end in an emotional battle where participants struggle to justify their positions. Having an open mind while keeping your eye on the prize is very important.

There is no single best way to approach a negotiation. The strategic choice should be the outcome of an analysis of the parties, their goals and the situation. Before entering a negotiation, the advantages and disadvantages of the opening with facts, rights, power, or interests should be evaluated.

- **Facts.** Discussing facts, rather than positions, can help identify the area of negotiation. In some cases, it is constructive to uncover the situation, the problems and also identify potential solutions together. Sometimes lack of agreement lies in the interpretation of the facts and not the facts themselves.

- **Rights.** Opening a negotiation by stating your rights framework can be a very strong and offensive opening. This could, however, encourage a defensive response, presenting an opposite interpretation of rights. In order to avoid this, it is recommended to refer to objective criteria, such as rules, laws, custom and standard order of business.

- **Power.** Opening a negotiation by establishing your power in the form of a threat or a take-it-or-leave-it offer could result in a very short negotiation. Your counterpart may understand that carrying out the threat requires an expenditure of your resources. He could walk away from the negotiation table, leaving you with the options to act on your threat or lose face. This is why it is better to issue a warning. This is done by making them imagine what would happen if you do not come to an agreement. People are usually motivated more by loss than by gain and, in most cases, imagination is more vivid than reality.

- **Interests.** There are not many risks when opening a negotiation by asking questions and focusing on understanding the other party's interests and underlying motives. By strategically sharing information, you could move forward to sharing interest-based proposals and solutions. Be careful not to overshare confidential information.

The anchoring effect

One of my clients, a freelance advisor in financial service, shared an interesting story with me. Under normal circumstances, his calendar is filled on average for seven to eight months in advance with consulting projects. He provides services all over the globe and thus frequently travels. When COVID-19 hit, a large part of the world went into lockdown, the first market response was a cancellation of all the onsite client meetings. His initial reaction to a clearing of the calendar was mild panic. In one day, he lost at least half of a year of financial security. A few weeks into lockdown, he received a request for proposal from a new client from eastern Europe. The project lay outside the scope of his usual advisory services and hence my client was not sure what to quote for it. Nonetheless, he was eager to prepare a good proposal in hopes of getting back in business. I suggested he schedule a follow-up call with the prospective client to find out a little bit more and perhaps figure out what the right opening offer should be. During the virtual meeting, the other party explained a bit more about similar projects and casually mentioned a range of what other consultants offer. My client called me immediately after and exclaimed: 'I now know what my opening offer should be!' Surprised by this rapid turnaround, I asked him how he had figured it out so quick. He replied that, 'this is what the other consultants quote'. He fell in the anchoring trap.

The anchoring effect is a perceptual illusion that occurs when we rely on the piece of information offered by the other party and allow it to serve as a reference point for our offering. This cognitive bias often takes place in the opening phase. An anchor does not have to be an explicit number or range, although it often is. Expectations can be set by mentioning important projects and activities, prominent clients, or even by choosing a specific (high-end) venue for the meeting or relying on attributes of status, such as fancy offices, accessories, dress code, and so on. The psychological power of an anchor is strong, because as social beings we are taught the rules of compliance and order. Going against these laws can feel uncomfortable and out of line. I am not suggesting a rebellious approach; however, it is necessary to exercise caution and double check whether their anchor resonates with yours.

As shown in the example of my client, the anchoring effect depends on the context, your attitude and the style of the counterpart. In situations of uncertainty and increased anxiety, you may become more suggestible, because you are governed by emotions rather than reason. It is helpful to seek a second objective opinion to make sure you are not anchoring in their waters.

Self-assessment – Can you identify all the anchors?

Dear Valued Partner,

In view of our ongoing partnership, we are sending you important information in preparation for our upcoming negotiations.

Due to volatile economic and political conditions that have impacted our business operations, we are currently restructuring our business by introducing the NEW HORIZONS project.

In appreciation of our partnership, we ask you to confirm in writing that you will refrain from price increases for your products in the next year.

Upon receipt of your confirmation, you will receive an official invitation to our negotiation meeting.

Best regards,
The Legal Department

▶

Self-assessment explanations:

Valued Partner – choice of words places you in a privileged position, you may fear to lose the status if you do not comply.

Ongoing partnership – implies there is a history and a potential for continuity, yet another factor that may trigger loss aversion.

Important information – draws your attention to the rank of the matter.

Our upcoming negotiations – statement of fact, not something under question or discussion.

Due to volatile economic and political conditions – this anchor works on three levels:

1 from the legal perspective: factors outside of the control of the other party, independent of their will (force majeure);

2 from the psychological perspective: providing an explanation increases the chances of acceptance more than just expressing a raw demand with no explanation;

3 an attempt to awaken empathy.

NEW HORIZONS – pulling you into their reality, their story; the uppercase characters signify importance and on the visual level catch the eye and therefore are easier engraved in the mind.

In appreciation of our partnership we ask you – implicit meaning: if you do not confirm in writing, this means you do not appreciate the relationship.

Upon receipt of your confirmation, you will receive an official invitation to our negotiation meeting – an invitation will only be possible if you confirm.

The Legal Department – this anchor works on two levels:

1 bringing in the legal team signifies that the matter is serious;

2 Department = de-personification of the sender. There is no individual responsibility nor contact person.

How should you react to the anchor?

Before responding it is essential that you identify who your contact person is and address your message directly to them. Keep it short, non-committal and respectful. Introduce *your* anchor. Propose an invitation agenda for the meeting. Here is how this could go:

Dear Ms Lawyer (name of the person),

▶

Thank you for your kind message.

We would be delighted to learn more about your project and tell you about our Green Strategy 2.0 project that we believe will help move our partnership forward.

We suggest a 30-minute meeting on . . . . at. . . ., alternatively on. . . at . . . . Which date would be more convenient for you?

We look forward to our ongoing cooperation.

Sincerely,

Your name and contact details

Who should open first?

One negotiation technique is never making the first offer because of the risk of 'showing your cards' and possibly giving away some of your leverage. Other real-life examples show that making the first offer can have a positive impact both on the task and on the relationship.

As discussed, the party making the first offer can gain an important advantage by opening the negotiation in their favour. The anchoring effect can also have a negative impact when the anchor is placed too high. This can result in the 'cooling' or the 'boomerang' effect. The 'cooling' effect refers to a party becoming disinterested in negotiating. The 'boomerang' effect refers to the counterparty making an equally 'extreme' offer. To minimise these risks, it is advised to make a first offer only when you have a thorough understanding of the market conditions and the other factors that will impact the other party's offer.

I tend to follow a simple rule in my negotiations. It takes into account two aspects: stakes and valuation. **If the stakes are fairly low for me (and I make sure they are by securing alternatives), and I want to test how the other side values me as a partner, I allow them to open first.** I perceive their opening offer as a test of our relationship. I am confident that the task part can in most cases be negotiated, but if the relational fundaments are not there, the agreement will not turn out to be mutually beneficial. Allowing them to open saves a lot of time in the future execution of the deal. After reading this book, you too will be strategically prepared to tackle the task-related aspects; therefore, you should be confident with allowing them to open first.

Expert view

Dan Staner
VP & Head of EMEA Region at Moderna, Switzerland

I usually open first. This allows me to shape the dialogue. The way I open is by trying to position what is at stake in the negotiation and by focusing on the two to three major axes from our perspective.

I do not talk about a solution, but rather focus on the theme which is at stake. Then the other party can come back and validate (or not), agree or not agree. Usually they add a few points from their side. I try to anchor around these points to find a common ground. This is how the discussions open.

Effect of opening offers

Many studies confirm that opening offers have a large impact on the final nego-tiated price. The opening offers are therefore one of the best predictors of the end result. Both research and practice show that very ambitious negotiators achieve better results than more modest ones. They can improve these results if they express a reflection of their ambition in the opening offer.

Factors that will have an impact on the opening offer are age, seniority, experi-ence, training, gender, culture (for example, negotiators from the United States indicated a strong likeliness to use exaggerating opening offers), preferences for risk, past experiences, psychological profile and attitude (confidence or lack thereof).

Designing the negotiation agenda

The negotiation agenda is one of the most influential structural aspects of the negotiation. It allows you to manage the flow and the pace of the process, to control the key targets for the different phases, as well as coordinate the activi-ties of the negotiating team.

The most important strategic issues that need to be taken into account when you prepare the negotiation agenda are the following.

1. Scope of the agenda

The pre-defined topic (objective) along with a list of issues that parties agree to discuss. In highly formal negotiations the agenda itself can be the result of prolonged negotiations. One of the telltales that you are dealing with a skilled negotiator is that they will strive to manage the agenda by either adding an item, limiting or extending the proposed agenda scope or time, or rejecting your agenda altogether. In that sense, agenda management can also be a tactic.

Agendas without a predefined subject (also defined as 'open boundary' agendas) that allow maximum flexibility increase the risk of unanticipated demands. When determining whether an agenda should be open or closed, you should consider that including certain issues will have effects. My recommendation is a closed agenda, because this allows you better control of the process.

2. Agenda sequence

Organising the issues under discussion in order of importance. There are different tactics regarding the placement. One rule states that earlier issues have greater importance and often also more time and energy are allocated to these. There are two possible approaches:

- The crescendo approach: The way that the topics are addressed is by increasing difficulty. With this approach negotiators can make some concessions early which will strengthen the sense of partnership. This will help when it comes to negotiating the more difficult points.

- The decrescendo approach: This method is the opposite of the crescendo approach. Instead of having the most sensitive point at the end of the list, it deals with it at the beginning. This approach is considered as higher risk, because it starts with addressing conflicting interests. The advantage is that you are being upfront and transparent with the other party.

3. Framing agenda items

The presentation of the issues as well as the language used to describe them can imply a willingness to cooperate or even show the negotiation power between the parties. Creating momentum in a negotiation is very important and therefore linking certain issues and creating an interdependence so that both parties can reach a consensus on these agenda items is a prerequisite to reaching an executable agreement.

Here are some tips on how to frame the items:

- Use positive verbs: For example, instead of ' Let us not waste this opportunity', use 'This is a great opportunity for us to explore'.
- Use future and action-oriented words.
- Do not present too many items. Three is a good number.
- Do not make the agenda too long or too detailed; state the most important points for discussion only (see agenda template in Figure 11.1 and the agenda sample).

4. Packaging of the agenda

There are different strategies revolving around package issues. Some negotiators prefer to discuss each item separately, while others try to fully understand the parameters of the negotiation and then proceed to negotiate several issues in a package. Practice shows that the latter approach allows a helicopter view of everything that is on the table and as such is recommended for high-stakes deals with multiple parameters.

5. Level of formality

The protocol depends on the relationship between the parties and the type of negotiation. In some negotiations it is important to develop a formal framework or guidelines to ensure common rules are in place. This is often the case for diplomatic or multiparty negotiations in an international setting.

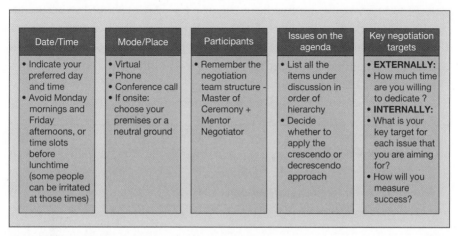

Date/Time	Mode/Place	Participants	Issues on the agenda	Key negotiation targets
• Indicate your preferred day and time • Avoid Monday mornings and Friday afternoons, or time slots before lunchtime (some people can be irritated at those times)	• Virtual • Phone • Conference call • If onsite: choose your premises or a neutral ground	• Remember the negotiation team structure - Master of Ceremony + Mentor Negotiator	• List all the items under discussion in order of hierarchy • Decide whether to apply the crescendo or decrescendo approach	• **EXTERNALLY:** • How much time are you willing to dedicate ? • **INTERNALLY:** • What is your key target for each issue that you are aiming for? • How will you measure success?

Figure 11.1 Agenda template

6. Time management

An agenda is a means of structuring not only the process, but also controlling how much time is invested in the process. The proper use of time, the length that is allocated to issues and how much time overall is given to the negotiation have to be compared to the return on the negotiation (RoN) when assessing what makes sense or not. Negotiation, like any other business activity, has a concrete cost, one of the greatest items of expenditure being time. It needs to be used wisely.

How to work out how much time you need:

Since three is the recommended number of agenda items, it would make sense to allocate approximately 20 to a maximum of 30 minutes per each. Naturally, the time may vary when issues are complex. Meetings that drag on for too long become counterproductive. Firstly, participants quickly lose the attention span. Secondly, they start going in circles around the same topic. A short and crisp meeting agenda focuses the attention due to a limitation of the duration.

Agenda template example

We would like to invite you to a meeting on Tuesday, the (insert date) at 10:30 am. The meeting will take place at (insert location). The participants will be Ms Jane Smith and Mr Adam Green (no need to disclose the role division of MC and MN to the other party). We would like to discuss the following items with you: scope of service, payment terms and length of contract. We propose having the meeting until noon. Thereafter, we would like to invite you to lunch together.

An important factor to keep in mind during the agenda is that there is no strictly right or wrong approach for the process. Parties should structure an agenda that suits them and works for them. The process can be adapted during the negotiation to create further opportunities for value creation. Regardless of the approach, it is highly advised to jointly agree on the agenda and the process before jumping in to the context.

Expert view

Anette Weber
Group CFO at Bucherer, Switzerland

Before you prepare an agenda for a negotiation, you need to be clear about what you want to achieve, where you can compromise and what are your alternative

▶

courses of action. If you are not alone in a negotiation, you also need to agree on the roles the particular people will play. However, your mindset towards the agenda should be flexible to be able to adapt to the changing dynamic and flow of the negotiation. The static element of the agenda relates to the task and role distribution. Once the tasks and roles are defined, everybody on the negotiation team should stick to them.

The purpose of the agenda setting is to avoid being taken off-guard and to understand derailers. Having a pre-determined plan and knowing your alternatives are important factors that can contribute to emotional balance. It is essential to keep calm and be aware of your trigger points. This requires a lot of self-reflection and ego control. People need to understand their roles both in relation to their individual inclinations and as part of the strategic placement in the negotiation process. Normally, a negotiation serves a higher purpose; it is not only about the negotiator and their interests.

Summary of key take-aways

1 The opening is a critical moment for establishing your position, building rapport with the other party and taking the lead of the process.

2 Be aware that the anchoring effect might impact your own perception.

3 You can craft an anchor and use it to strengthen the allure of your offering.

4 In deciding whether to open first use the following rule: If the stakes are fairly low for you, and to test how the other side values you, allow them to open first.

5 Be the one who designs, proposes and manages the agenda.

Further reading

1 Carnevale, P.J. (2019) Strategic time in negotiation. *Current Opinion in Psychology* 26, 106–112.

2 Lytle, A.L., Brett, J.M. and Shapiro, D.L. (1999) *The Strategic Use of Interests, Rights, and Power to Resolve Disputes*. Plenum Publishing Corporation.

3 Patton, C. and Balakrishnan, P.V. (Sundar) (2012) *Negotiating When Outnumbered: Agenda Strategies for Bargaining with Buying Teams*. Elsevier B.V.

4   Pendergast, W.R. (1990) Managing the negotiation agenda. *Negotiation Journal* 6, 135–145.

5   Pon Staff (2021) Negotiation Techniques: The First Offer Dilemma in Negotiations. 25 January 2021.

6   Pon Staff (2019) The Anchoring Effect and How It Can Impact Your Negotiation. 26 November 2019. Shonk, K. (2021) Negotiation Advice: When to Make the First Offer in Negotiation. Harvard Law School. 30 March 2021.

7   Van Poucke, D. and Buelens, M. (2002) *Predicting the Outcome of a Two-party Price Negotiation: Contribution of Reservation Price, Aspiration Price and Opening Offer.* Elsevier Science B.V.

8   Wheeler, M. (2014) *Anxious Moments: Openings in Negotiations.* Blackwell Publishing.

9   Wu, H.D. and Colman, R. (2009) Advancing agenda-setting theory: the comparative strength and new contingent conditions of the two levels of agenda-setting effects. *J&MC Quarterly* 86 (4) Winter.

CHAPTER 12
SUCCESSFULLY EXECUTING THE DEALING PHASE

'You must not only aim right, but draw your bow with all your might.'

Henry David Thoreau

What you will discover in this chapter:

- How to prepare your demands and prioritise them
- How to present your demands, which words to use and which to avoid
- How to react when you receive counter-demands
- Answers to the most common questions about the dealing phase

The heart of the matter

Demands are the concrete asks that you bring to the table. These requests constitute the negotiation mass and serve as your chips for trade in a negotiation. When formulating demands you need to refer back to your negotiation mission and your G–T–O (goal, target and objective). For some negotiators, the word 'demand' may be perceived as too harsh, pushy or, well, . . . demanding. If you are not fully comfortable with the linguistic choice, there are a few other substitutes you can use: asks, requests, requirements or expectations. For the purpose of consistency with the topic of High-Impact negotiations, I am using the noun 'demand'.

The dealing phase constitutes the heart of the negotiation process. In this stage the negotiators exchange demands in the quest for reaching their objectives.

Explicitly asking for something can cause stress levels to rise. Dealing is the most operational part, because it is primarily oriented to the task realisation. One of the frequent pitfalls that negotiators make is that they limit their vision only to the task. As a result, some practitioners struggle to quickly get the dealing over with. Here are some of the commonly shared concerns.

- How to get what I want without being forceful, being less direct, not to come across as harsh or pushy.
- Discovering the hidden motives of the other party.
- Goals misalignment on the external level.
- Understanding the goal of the other party when they don't disclose their cards.

Looking at the comments, it is clear that the focus is narrowed down to the technical aspects and is often one-sided. However, the feedback also indicates that there is a second level disguised in the form of hidden agendas that lead to misalignment between the goals of the negotiators.

In order to overcome the internal anxiety and potential threat to the partnership that a mishandled dealing phase can cause, it is recommended to make sure that both parties share a mutual understanding of the negotiation process. If both acknowledge that the dealing phase is the moment that demands are exchanged, then the act of asking will no longer be perceived as forceful or demanding. Recognition of the give-and-take nature of the process is the condition for a more cooperative dynamic.

Exchange of demands

Unskilled negotiators tend to bring down the dealing to the unilateral voicing of demands. Instead, it should feel like a natural next step on your path towards agreement. You can even make it fun and creative. I like to compare this phase to cooking something up out of ingredients that you both bring to the table. This idea takes me back to when I was on a scholarship in the south of France. The monthly grant was rather modest. The less you have, the more innovative you become, especially when it comes to finding ways to satisfy your basic needs. Our daily cooking ritual was a meet up in the cafeteria. Each student would bring the few ingredients they happened to have in their fridge. We would then spread them out on the table and assess what we could cook that night. Surprisingly, we always had great food and an unforgettable time.

Hierarchy of demands

Earlier in this book we compared the negotiation landscape to a picture frame. The borders are designated by the maximum and the minimum target that you want to achieve, as shown in Figure 12.1. The demands constitute what is referred to as the negotiation mass, or the cooking dough if we are to use the metaphor for the cake you want to bake. The recipe for a successful negotiation is having a hierarchy of the ingredients. Some carry more and some less weight.

There are four types of demands that you need to prepare.

1 Heavyweight – the things you **must** achieve to reach your target (the deal-breakers).

2 Middleweight – the things you **should** achieve.

3 Lightweight – the things you **could** achieve (the items for concession-making).

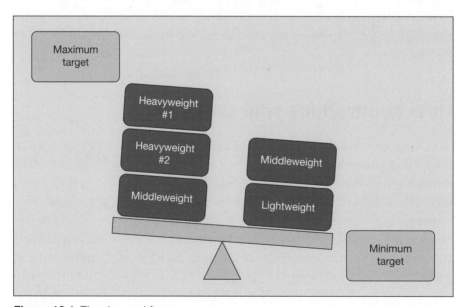

Figure 12.1 The demand frame

4 The non-negotiables – such as your negotiation culture, personal and corporate standards, your values and belief system, the overall negotiation mission; in short, the intangibles that add non-monetary value but build up your goodwill and personal branding.

Having a hierarchy is a strategic control tool. It will allow you to monitor how you are doing in relation to reaching your aspirational goals. It is therefore a way of assessing progress. Furthermore, grouping your demands in categories will help you reach a decision as to which concessions you can make. Naturally, you should hold on to the heavyweight ones and sacrifice the middle- and lightweight first. A good tip is to leave a lightweight demand for the end of a negotiation, as a token of appreciation for the other party. Your aim is to give them the illusion of victory and a sense of recognition of their efforts. Those who feel like winners are more likely to implement the terms of the deal and cherish the relationship.

The list of demands will vary depending on the negotiation. Below are a few examples of typical demands that can serve as a source of inspiration. The category is not defined because it will be tailored to the maximum and minimum target of the deal.

Examples: Payment terms, length of deal, MOQ (minimum order quantity), choice of law, specific terms and conditions, penalties for non-compliance, risk sharing, division of roles and responsibilities, warranties, sales volume, quality standards and so on.

How to introduce your demands

Be careful how you word the demands. I remember one interesting moment during a bilingual negotiation between English- and French-speaking parties. The discussions involved the set-up of a sister company of the London firm which was to be based in Paris. The meetings were held in the French capital. Everything was going smoothly until the negotiation reached the dealing phase. Much to my surprise, in the middle of the meeting one of the English partners abruptly stood up from the table, thanked the French team and left the room. A coffee break was immediately called for. The person who had left was in the corridor outside the meeting room. When asked what caused such behaviour, the response was that he cannot deal with the arrogant French people any longer.

The moderator of the discussion was bilingual. The linguistic capacity proved a handicap in this case, because they missed the linguistic subtleties of word-for-word translation. It was only then that they realised that the word that the French team were frequently using was 'demander'. In French this verb means: to ask for. When translated literally, as in I demand a break, I demand to have my coffee and croissant, I demand to know what the agenda is, it can indeed come across as pushy. When the combination of the neutral 'demands' clashed with the actual asks, it was a bit too much to handle. The table below lists things to 'Do' and 'Don't'.

Do	Don't
<ul><li>*We require*</li><li>*We expect*</li><li>*We find it necessary* – assertive perspective</li><li>*We need the following steps going forward*</li><li>*Here are the points on the path to our agreement*</li></ul>	<ul><li>Not too many variations of verbs. If you variate too much on the verbal level, the other party may decode your hierarchy. The risk with that is that when you exchange a lightweight demand and ask for a higher value in return, they might be resistant to the trade due to unequal value.</li><li>*We allow* – you are not in a position to allow or disallow, both parties should feel like they are on the same level.</li><li>Asking for permission – you are not in a submissive position.</li><li>*Discuss later* – demands are not items up for discussion, but rather concrete asks.</li><li>*It is necessary* – objective perspective.</li></ul>
<ul><li>*Payment terms will be* – no discussion, framing as a statement of fact</li></ul>	<ul><li>*We would just like to ask for* – avoid minimisers, such as 'just', 'only', 'little point'.</li><li>*It is really important for us* – don't overemphasise the importance or display the hierarchy of the demand.</li><li>*We would really like to have, we really need* – get rid of the 'really'.</li><li>Anything soft and vague.</li><li>Anything suggesting openness to discussion from the moment you introduce the demand.</li></ul>

Do	Don't

• *This is the list of our asks and claims* + list them. For example: I want to build a house. I will need the following:
  • 1 ton of bricks
  • 2 tons of wood
  • 1 year for the construction
  • 2 reliable architects
  • 2 construction teams, etc.
	• *I think it would be fair* – subjective, avoid the concept of fairness altogether.
	• Not having any visuals – anything stated in writing and displayed in full view will be retained more than the fleeting verbal message.
	• Share screen option to display the demand list and to take the focus off the person presenting the demands (makes them more comfortable, because they are not in the spotlight).

• *We want* vs *We would like* – culture determines which form is used. Americans will be comfortable with the former, the British might prefer the latter	• *Suggest, propose* – you are not suggesting, you are asking for something. • *It would be good, nice to have* – wishful thinking, be more concrete.
• Be confident without being arrogant	• Over-selling the benefits to the other party – you are negotiating, not selling.
• Maintain a friendly and open pose	• Placing yourself in a submissive role.
• Be clear, precise and to the point	• Providing justifications, arguments to explain why you are making the demands (argument overkill) – will make the other party question why you need/deserve what you are requesting.
• Control your voice – the tone, pitch, speed, intonation, breathing patterns	• *It would be helpful if you gave us* – do not count on philanthropy, ask instead.
• Pay attention to your unconscious non-verbals, such as touching your chin, fixing your hair, and any other behaviours that may suggest nervousness or uneasiness.	• *It would be of interest to you* – let them be the judge of that. • *I would like to highlight the topic* – suggests a discussion rather than placing an ask • *It would be great if there was a possibility* – too idealistic. • *Do you have any questions?* OR • *What do you think?* OR • *Are you ok with this?* – invitation to counter immediately, risk of opening Pandora's box. Instead, you can thank them for their attention and wait for their counter-demands.

How to act when you receive counter-demands

1   Thank your negotiation partner for sharing their *view*. Avoid the word 'demand' to not reinforce the ask.

2   Do not pose this question: 'Is this your (final) position?' The only answer to that question is: yes. What it will cause is that the other party will dig their heels in their position to save face.

3   Do not repeat their exact demand, specifically avoid the numbers, such as the discount amount or the salary number. Repetition will legitimise it.

4   Check how the demands relate to your overall negotiation goal. In the heat of the dealing phase many negotiators lose sight of what their initial goal was.

5   Check your numbers carefully – assess the impact of their demands on your target – will it get you closer to your desired (maximum) target or will it bring you lower to the minimum target?

6   Consider if the list of demands resonates with your objective.

7   Take time before you respond or commit, at a minimum a 'coffee' break, ideally 'sleep on it' (an overnight cool-off period).

8   Understand that not committing includes making sure that you or your team do not communicate by para-verbal (the way you respond) or non-verbal cues (the way your body acts).

Most common questions about the dealing phase

Many business professionals encounter similar challenges when they enter the dealing phase. Below is a compilation of the typical questions posed by other negotiators along with answers and explanations of the logic behind each of them

Who should introduce their demands first?

You. The condition for this is that you have placed yourself in the position of the host of the negotiation since the very beginning. You initiated the design of the process, made the other party feel like they are part of it; you sent out the agenda, took care of creating the right atmosphere and created the illusions of autonomy and choice for them. Once this is done, your negotiation partner will already subconsciously be in the follower mode; therefore when it comes to dealing, it will be natural for them that you continue to take the lead.

Should you disclose the hierarchy of your demands?

No. The demand placing boils down to an exchange. You are not only trading tangible assets, but also non-tangibles, the most important of which is value. Value is strictly subjective and as such both parties will have differing understanding of what is precious and what is not. You need to make it seem like everything that you give away (in exchange for something) is valuable; otherwise, it will be taken for granted. If you disclose the value hierarchy then you strip yourself from the allure that value has.

Which demands should you start with?

You have two choices in this regard. A bit similar to the crescendo and decrescendo approach related to the opening offer, you can either start with the lightweight demands, and then move to the more important ones or address the heavyweight first. The advantage of the first strategy is that you warm your negotiation partner up to the bigger demands. Starting off with the heavyweights serves transparency and time efficiency. The other party knows from the get-go what your asks are. My recommendation is to kick off with the latter approach only when you have established a solid relationship of trust and have mutually agreed on the process so that the element of surprise has been alleviated. Otherwise, they may feel threatened or pushed into a corner.

Is a concession the same thing as compromise?

No. A compromise is a win–lose and a lose–win strategy. A concession is a demand that you grant in exchange for obtaining another demand that has more value for you.

How many demands should you prepare?

On average the number should not be less than ten. This amount will allow you to set up the hierarchy of importance and give you enough room for making concessions. This may increase depending on the complexity of the deal.

Practical tip: Double the number in the preparation phase, namely, come up with twice as many demands as you will present to the other party. Then, right before the meeting, slice it down to half. Many negotiators struggle with coming up with a list of demands and then presenting them in a confident manner. The slice-down technique will help you deal with both these challenges. Firstly, you will notice that it is possible to think of enough demands. Secondly, reduction of the points on your list will make you feel like you are asking almost for nothing. It is better to 'negotiate down' with yourself rather than with the other party.

What should be the percentage of heavy-, middle- and lightweight demands?

Assuming you prepare a minimum of ten demands, you should have approximately two or three heavy and two lightweight ones, while the rest are middleweight demands.

Should you present the demands one by one or in a bundle?

Presenting the demand list in its entirety and then listening to the presentation of the other party's list is the preferred structure. If you go on a demand-by-demand basis, then you risk getting stuck discussing one particular ask. This increases the risk of developing tunnel vision, a narrowing of focus. A bundle approach allows you to gain an oversight of all the ingredients on the table before you get to the cooking.

Should the demands be visually disclosed?

Yours should be disclosed and left in full sight for the other party to look at as long as possible. In virtual meetings you can use the share screen option, present your list of demands and then schedule a discussion or a coffee break with the screen on share mode. In live meetings, you can write them down on a flipchart that you will put in a position that the other party will be looking at all the time. Alternatively, you can use a whiteboard, provided it is not in constant use and will not be erased quickly.

Do not write down their exact demands, so that you are not primed by them.

Whose demands should I or my team prepare – ours or theirs?

This is a question often posed by service providers. They are so client-oriented that they often neglect their own goals in the service of the other. This mindset transcends into the negotiation approach. The dealing phase is the moment in which *you* ask for what you need. The other party will surely do the same. This is the time to focus on the task more than the relationship. If a solid foundation in the form of agreement on the process is in place, this will not have a negative impact on the interpersonal dynamic. Quite the contrary, people admire someone who knows their worth and how to ask for what they need.

Who should present the demands?

The master of ceremony in charge of the negotiation (the speaking negotiator). This person needs to be confident and assertive but not arrogant.

What you see and what you don't

Many sources limit the dealing phase to the exchange of demands only. This approach fails to take into account the broader outlook, specifically what the reason is for the asks. On the strategic level, the demands are a means of reaching your targets. On a deeper level, there is always a cause for the target itself. That underlying factor is what is referred to as an interest or motive. Think of it like an iceberg. The demand is what you see above the waterline. The position – what the other party communicates they want – is expressed by that demand. What lies below the line of visibility are the reasons for why they want something – the interests and hidden motives. Usually interests reflect the problem and the basic challenge of a negotiation lies in the conflict between the side's need, concerns, desires and fears. The iceberg approach is presented in Figure 12.2.

How can you identify interests?

- Ask 'Why?' – put yourself in their shoes and try to see the situation from their perspective; what would be arguments in favour of the deal?
- Ask 'Why not?' and think about their alternative choices;

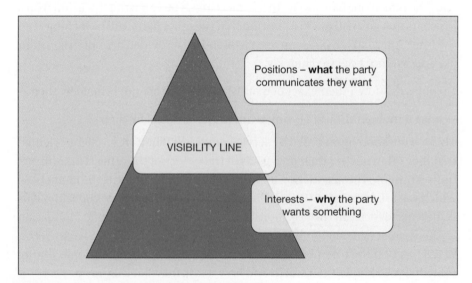

Figure 12.2 Positions and interests: the iceberg approach

- Realise that each side has many different interests, some of which may be conflicting, for example agent-principle or ethical dilemmas;
- Identify the most powerful needs – the basic human needs:
  - safety and security
  - economic well-being
  - a sense of belonging
  - recognition
  - need for control.

The principled approach to negotiation suggests focusing on interests rather than positions. Since positions are a reflection of interests, the two should not be separated nor one given priority over the other. A singular focus on motives while excluding positions can be counterproductive. One of the underlying critiques of the distinction between positions and interests relies on the outdated distinction between motivation and cognition. Many studies have been able to confirm that conflict may be related to cognitive differences and not just to conflicting interests. The relation between cognition and motivation has been a matter of controversy in psychology for a long time and it seems reasonable to believe that motivation is not completely reducible to cognition. When different parties have opposed motives, that may lead to conflict. Nevertheless, it is also true that conflict can result from different ways of seeing the world. In such cases it is hard to distinguish between interests and positions since both are inextricably entwined. People's identities and interests are closely bound up with the positions that they take on issues. The idea of interests and positions always being distinguishable rests on the assumption that human behaviour can always be explained by drives or instincts, which is not the case.

In many situations the concept of focusing on interests rather than positions might be a useful reminder to try and seek out the underlying causes of conflict. However, this approach is sometimes difficult to apply because it often oversimplifies or hides the real dynamics of the conflict. It may also carry a bias against one party, where the unity of a party is considered dependent on a unified position. The attractiveness for searching a party's interest is the genuine merit of seeking out the motivation and objective interests. Instead of emphasising the distinction between positions and interests, it may be more useful to alert negotiators to focusing on the underlying issues enrobed as a demand. Your role is to uncover both the why behind the what in order to understand how best to exchange the demands.

Expert view

Alexander Kostecki
Founder & COO at Clair, USA

The interests that drive the behaviour of your negotiation partner are actually the cracks of a negotiation. Your goal is to equip yourself with as much information as possible. I see interest identification as a two-phase process that happens in the pre-negotiation preparation and the actual negotiation.

I never approach an important deal without preparation. This includes the following steps.

1 I speak to the other party's customers to understand what points were most difficult to obtain in the negotiation, and what were the sticking points.

2 I always model out the economics of a contract and run sensitivities to look for the effect of risk aversion.

3 I test the strategy of my negotiation tactic on simiiar (but less desirable) partners first before I present the strategy to the negotiation partner I am targeting. More importantly, I always negotiate across multiple alternatives!

In the negotiation phase I have an open conversation on how the other party feels about the deal (term, variability, long-term strategy, and so on). I always open with a conversation about them, I prolong their perspective-taking process and give them space without saying yes or no. In the background, I am usually running 10–15 discussions with other prospects to see what the recurring theme is, to test the pain threshold and find a match point.

Summary of key take-aways

1 Agree on the process before you introduce the demands.

2 Present your demands first, then listen to the list of the other party.

3 Prepare a hierarchy of demands and categorise them according to heavy-, middle- and lightweight and do not omit the non-negotiable items.

4 Be careful how you word your demands.

5 Uncover the hidden interests behind the demands.

Further reading

1   Brehmer, B. and Hammond, K.R. (1977) Cognitive factors in interpersonal conflict. *Negotiations: Social-psychological Perspectives* (edited by D. Druckman). Beverly Hills: Sage.

2   Loewenstein, J. and Howell, T. (2010) Understanding and using what we want: interests and exploitation in negotiations. 23rd Annual International Association of Conflict Management.

3   Pfeffer, J. (1992) *Managing with Power: Politics and Influence in Organizations*. Boston: Harvard Business School Press.

4   Provis, C. (1996) Interests vs. positions: a critique of the distinction. *Negotiation Journal* October 1996.

5   Senger, J.M. (2002) *Tales of the Bazaar: Interest-Based Negotiation Across Cultures*. Plenum Publishing Corporation.

6   Shell, G.R. (2010) The morality of bargaining: identity versus interests in negotiations with evil. *Negotiation Journal* 26 (4), 453–481.

CHAPTER 13
CLOSING THE DEAL

'The course of true love never did run smooth.'

William Shakespeare
A Midsummer Night's Dream

What you will discover in this chapter:

- How to know when it makes sense to close and when it does not
- Tips for closing the deal
- The major challenges that you can encounter at the closing phase

To close or not to close?

Contrary to what some business professionals think, a negotiation does not end with a deal being signed. It is concluded when the negotiated terms can be implemented and there is a potential for a lasting business relationship between the parties. Deal-makers equate closing with securing a signature on the dotted line. Signed paperwork and ticked-off formalities do not necessarily translate into executable agreements; especially in some cultures this may not be worth much. Real-makers are those negotiators who recognise and seize untapped business opportunities by working on two levels. They understand that a working agreement needs to bridge the execution of the task and solidify the established relationship in the long term.

You have made it this far and you are now equipped to become a real-maker – a negotiator who not only closes the deal, but also makes sure that the terms of the agreement are implementable. You know how to define the mission statement, set the goal, establish the objective, gather the necessary information, choose the best approach, create the right environment, take the lead, open and execute the negotiation, all the while adding value to the process both from the task and the relational perspective.

There are two possibilities of ending the negotiation: agreement and no agreement. Both are valid. It is worth pointing out that no agreement does not equal disagreement. No agreement means that at this particular point in time, based on the demands that were exchanged and the information that was shared, it does not make sense to close.

The question then is why are there so many foul and non-executable deals? Perhaps the perspective theory elaborated by Nobel-Prize winner Daniel Kahneman in collaboration with Amos Tversky can shed some light on this. According to the researchers, loss aversion is a stronger motivator than gain. Awareness of this psychological phenomenon should serve as a screening mechanism the next time you are tempted to prematurely close a deal just because you invested time, energy and resources in the process.

Four ways for assessing when it makes sense to close

1 **When you have met or exceeded your negotiation goal and objective and reached your target.**
   How to assess this:

   ● Go back to your initial goal and objective. Assess whether you can clearly and positively answer the *what for?* question.

   ● Check your financial figures that constitute your target. Are you within the maximum and minimum limits you set for the negotiation?

2 **When the new deal is 'better' than the status quo (the overall conditions existing before the deal)**
   How to assess this:

   ● A 'better' deal can be measured by a strengthening of the relationship between the parties. Is there potential for a long-lasting partnership and repeated business? Can you trust the other party to carry out the negotiated terms? Are they someone you want to be bound by an agreement with? – If you answered 'no' to any of these questions, then re-think the closing.

- What type of precedence does the deal create? Any agreement will create a specific future expectation based on past performance (in psychology, this is referred to as a perceptual set). For example, if you created a pattern where you compromised a lot, the other party will expect that this will be the case for any next negotiations that may follow.

- What type of negotiation culture will the deal create? You become what you do. Although there is merit in not discussing morality, you might consider whether the end justifies the means. If you need to sacrifice your non-negotiables (both tangible and intangible), it might be best not to close.

3 **When the RoN (Return on Negotiation) is positive**
How to assess this:

- Sum up the time and resources dedicated to the deal and compare your result with the expected return. Do the benefits outweigh the costs?

- To give you a rough idea how much organisational time is locked up (as opportunity or sunk costs) in a negotiation, do this exercise: The next time you start a negotiation process, open an Excel sheet. In the file, mark down every hour that you dedicate to the negotiation (both internal and external discussions). Have every member involved in the negotiation team mark their hours. At the end of the week count all the hours and multiply them by the average hourly work rate. You will be amazed by what you will discover.

4 **When you have slept on it**
How to assess this:

- Do not commit to closing the deal immediately after you finish the negotiation. Give yourself a cool-off moment. This should be not less than one night.

- Does the deal look rosy the next morning? If so, go ahead with the agreement.

Ideally, all four points should be met. However, it may happen that you might not manage to reach your target (point 1) or have a positive RoN (point 3), but the deal has a potential for a future positive yield through a new promising partnership or establishment of a strong negotiation goodwill. In such a situation, you may temporarily compromise on the financial aspects. Point 4 is non-negotiable. Always sleep on it before you make any binding decision.

When is it better not to conclude the deal?

Some authors suggest that you should always negotiate if there is a small chance that you might gain something valuable from engaging, even with your enemies. I do not agree with that nor with the statement that 'you can negotiate anything'. Some things are non-negotiable and there are people with whom and circumstances under which you should not do business.

First of all, you should compare the expected costs and benefits to see if closing makes sense. In case of a tie between pragmatism and ego after performing a cost–benefit analysis, pragmatism should win. When the decision is made on behalf of others, make sure that you do not let your own moral intuitions or personal interests override a pragmatic assessment of the deal.

It is worthwhile to get advice from multiple people when you evaluate the alternatives to closing. This will allow you to resist the temptation of closing based on your subjective perceptions, biases, intuitive judgements and emotional attachment.

Tips to close the deal

The next thing that you will have to do once you have assessed that it makes sense to close the deal is to make sure that the end of the process does not ruin all the efforts you have made during the negotiation phases. You certainly want to avoid the winner's dance. Instead, downplay your own victory and give the impression to the other party that they are getting a great (better than their *status quo*) deal with you. Here are some tips that will help you close efficiently and elegantly.

1 Stick to your guns
   • If you prepared, assessed the situation properly and you feel like the deal you are offering will add value for both sides, then move in for the close.

2 Let them talk
   • Give them space to express their opinion and expectations. You might uncover potential obstacles that may hinder the execution of the deal.

3   Do not pressure

- In the closing phase, the other party can start having second thoughts. This is natural. Do not push them to close, otherwise they might become suspicious or defensive. Gently remind them of the value that the deal brings to them.

- It is important to not put into place tight deadlines as this could have a negative impact on the relationship. Instead, you can create a sense of urgency by showing the other party what they might miss out on if they hesitate too long.

4   Show your credibility

- To make the deal more realistic and achievable, you can refer to past cases to help the other party understand what works for you and what does not, and how you operate. Reference to past deals in your portfolio shows you have experience and are a credible partner.

5   Mitigate risk

- Make the deal as simple to implement as possible for the other party and eliminate any downside risks for them.

6   Agree on a joint summary

- Never end the negotiation with your own summary. Make sure that you and your negotiation partner are on the same page when you close. The joint summary can expose some open issues. Expect a re-negotiation to shut all the open doors before you close the whole deal.

7   Build them a golden bridge

- In order for a deal to be implementable, you must secure the buy-in of the other party. The condition for that is two-fold. They must feel good about the process (and the end result), and they must feel good about themselves. Avoid loss of face of the other party and make them feel like winners who cross the bridge towards agreement out of their own free will.

8   Learn to walk away

- Although this may sound counter-intuitive, if while closing the deal you still feel like the other party is going for a one-sided win instead of a mutually beneficial agreement, then do not be afraid to politely offer to discontinue the deal.

Expert view

Dr Daniel Schönfelder
Vice President at Battery Materials (BASF SE), Europe

From the retrospective view, there might be different interests depending on whether we want to negotiate to primarily close a deal or negotiate to ultimately implement it. This consideration will change the outlook on the whole negotiation process. I use the 'implementability' factor as a benchmark to assess whether the deal I am negotiating will be the best one when the moment comes to execute it. 'Is this something we can actually execute?' is a very helpful question that should be addressed. Otherwise concessions may be made for the sake of closing a deal. If you look at the consequences through the lens of implementation, it may change your positioning and strategy. It may turn out that the combination of elements and concessions may not be the most beneficial for the execution of the deal.

If you fail to take into account how a deal can be executed, you run the risk of over-complicating certain terms in the course of the negotiation that might impair bringing the deal into life. Practicability and the ease of implementation are important factors that need to be assessed. The end result should be meaningful and reasonable. The consequences are also the best filters for ego and power plays. The trick is to get the right proportion between negotiation and the execution of the agreement. Over-focus on the success of the deal may come at the expense of executing it in practice. The closing vs implementation ratio should be carefully balanced.

The major challenges at the closing phase

The closing phase needs to be handled with particular care. Seeing the end on the horizon and an anticipation of crowning of the efforts can leave some negotiators blind to the issues that can still surface in the last rounds. Here are the typical roadblocks that you need to be aware of.

1   **Heavyweight demand:** The other party may have been feeding you light-weight demands during the whole negotiation and then decide to bring out the heavyweight demand at the end. You risk falling out of your negotiation frame (the limits designated by the maximum and minimum target), and not reaching your objective.

What to do: Make it known that a heavyweight demand that risks destabilising the whole process ultimately means a re-start of the process. This is not a re-negotiation of the terms, but a new negotiation – with new demands that you will bring to the table once you re-align your negotiation objective and target.

2   **Entry of a new player:** The appearance of a new persona in the negotiation will inevitably change the dynamic between the existing parties. This can be a skilled professional, a negotiator of a different status (usually higher in the hierarchy for effect) or a person of a different gender, age or experience. All these factors will impact the energy between the existing relationship.

What to do: Be careful to carefully assess, at the start of the process, who has the authority to negotiate and whether closing the deal will require the presence of any other parties. Agree to the set up in writing. One of the common pitfalls is negotiating with the wrong party who does not have the license to close the deal.

3   **Hardball tactics:** Your negotiation partner probably knows that you are eager to close the deal. Therefore, they may use power tactics, apply pressure, deadlines, threats or other manipulation tactics.

What to do: Make it immediately known that you do not operate under threats. Clearly set the boundaries of what you accept and what you do not. Do not comply. This is not the environment in which you should agree to making compromises.

4   **Disrupted communication** – also referred to as 'ghosting'. You get to the closing and suddenly the other party goes quiet.

What to do: The occurrence of periods of silence should be managed at the start. You can for example agree that if you do not get a reply within a certain timeframe, this is equivalent to implicit agreement. If that has not been done, then you can follow up, but only once. Show you care without over-caring. Although this may sound extreme, there is always the option of walking away. You should seriously consider whether someone who ghosts you is the type of person whom you can trust with implementation of the deal. Sometimes it is better to walk away than to throw good money after bad.

5   **Bad timing:** You can have a great deal, but it can come at the wrong time. Do not fight with *force majeure* (events in the life cycle of the negotiation beyond

your direct control). Although you should strategically plan and execute the negotiation process, leave a margin of flexibility for the unknown and let things take their flow, even if that means not closing in the exact moment you planned to.

What to do: Leave a possibility of re-entry open for yourself and your negotiation partner. Today and due to the existing circumstances, you decide not to close, but you nonetheless leave a door open in case momentum is better in the future.

6   **Not asking for the close:** If they still want to negotiate in the closing phase, this means there is an interest. The simple test is the question: Are they still communicating with you?

What to do: Don't be afraid to ask for the close, even if to see if you are reasonably close to wrapping up the deal.

7   **Incompatible deal options or irreconcilable differences between the parties:** An implementable and long-lasting deal is a marriage between the task-oriented and the relational aspects that make up the negotiation. If you are striving for deal-making longevity, you need to make sure that by closing you secure both these elements.

What to do: Go back to the **four benchmarks for assessing when it makes sense to close** that we discovered earlier in the chapter. Do not close for the sake of closing.

Expert view

Sean Whitley
Vice President of Sales at Mitto, USA

The major challenge is thinking that your value is aligned with the expectations of your negotiation partner. Salespeople and negotiators involved in high-stakes deals have what we refer to as 'happy ears'. What this basically means is that they hear what they want to hear. For example, they only focus on the positive buying signals in an intro call. However, if you do not identify whether 'they have the juice', a good call or initial discussion does not guarantee you will get a signature on the dotted line. The main issue is therefore not overshooting reality. Particularly in the closing phase, you have to be a realist. You need to ask yourself the question whether your negotiation partner is happy enough to move the deal forward or are you just being

▶

biased. It is challenging to read the situation properly, to be objective and step out of your own paradigm of understanding.

On the strategic level, you can have another negotiator entering the scene in the eleventh hour who risks blowing up the deal. This may be a tactic or simply a turn of events, such as when the procurement team changes, and the new decision maker does not give the green light for the deal. This may restart the negotiation process. It can also happen that a deal-breaking item appears on the table in the closing phase. This might prolong the process, but the negotiator must ensure that the partnership moves forward.

The psychological side effects of closing

Successfully concluding a negotiation will give you a confidence boost. Conversely, this can have a negative impact on your next deal-making. The emotions that you have post negotiation have a spill-over effect. As much as we would like to put these emotions aside during our next negotiation and be rational, it is very difficult to eliminate them. For professionals who go from one negotiation to another, this can have a significant impact on the ego. Pride and over-confidence are not desirable traits of a negotiator. Experiments show that people (typically male negotiators) who succeeded in their negotiation did not perform well in the next ones and vice versa. To mitigate the risks of the ego boost it is recommended to take breaks between subsequent negotiations, pinpoint the source of the emotion and strive for a humble mindset.

Negotiators addicted to the winner's high can suffer from the inability to reject a deal, even if it is suboptimal. Learning to walk away is a valuable skill. Nonetheless, negotiators sometimes struggle with allowing themselves to perceive it as a legitimate option. They stay in the negotiation, because they already invested time and effort in the process. They conclude suboptimal deals for the sake of closing. By doing so, they are unconsciously paving the way for future failure. Lingering on in an unfavourable situation is how you develop a perceptual set. This phenomenon occurs when you interpret a future situation through your past experiences and act similarly to how you did before. If your past is a pattern of settling for less, you are likely to transplant that behaviour to your future dealings. To avoid this, give yourself the right not to close anything less than the best deal. By doing so, you may be actually winning.

Summary of key take-aways

1 Negotiation is concluded when the negotiated terms can be implemented and there is a potential for a lasting business relationship between the parties.

2 Both agreement and no agreement are valid ways of ending a negotiation.

3 Compare the expected costs and benefits to see if closing makes sense.

4 In case of a tie between pragmatism and ego after performing a cost–benefit analysis, pragmatism should win.

5 Do not allow the end on the horizon and the temptation to close the deal to blur your judgement of the issues that can surface in the last rounds.

Further reading

1 Closing a deal? Eight negotiation tactics to ensure a positive outcome. Forbes. 10/05/2021.

2 *Closing the Deal in Negotiations: 3 Tips for Sequential Dealmaking.* Harvard Law School. 09/11/2021.

3 *Masterful Negotiating* (2004), 2nd edn. Harvard Business Review.

4 Richemond, K. (2010) Closing the sale: The power of Negotiating to Win (Chapter 12). *The Power of Selling.* Saylor Foundation.

5 Techniques for improving your negotiating ability. *Negotiation Daily.* 31/08/2021.

CHAPTER 14
KEEPING THE MOMENTUM AFTER THE NEGOTIATION

'A great person attracts great people and knows how to hold them together.'

Johann Wolfgang Von Goethe

What you will discover in this chapter:

- How to evaluate whether the negotiation was successful
- How to move forward post negotiation
- How to carry out Negotiation Relationship Management (NRM)
- What to do after a negotiation that does not end with a deal

How to evaluate whether the negotiation was successful

Closing of a negotiation is the end of the beginning. Since the dynamic of every negotiation is different, you will discover something new each time you negotiate. To fully maximise the learning experience, you will now need to evaluate and monitor the results to improve for next time.

Since we established that the success of a negotiation aimed at reaching a sustainable agreement (as opposed to a one-off deal) is the balance between the task and the relationship, we can start by assessing the performance of the master of the ceremony – the negotiator. Why is this important? The negotiator is the business card of the company and the mouthpiece for the execution of its negotiation mission. The appointment of a negotiator is similar to filling any other organisational role. The person to job fit is of paramount importance. The negotiator of choice needs to possess a specific skillset (see Chapter 10) combined with the right personality type. Evaluating the results of the negotiation through the lens of the performance of the negotiator will allow you to make better placement decisions for future negotiations.

To track the progress of the negotiator, you should monitor what the negotiator does before, during and after the negotiation. You can rate their performance using a scale of 1–5 for each of the below questions (1 is bad, 5 is good):

- How well were they prepared?
- To what extent did they maximise the benefits of the counterparty as opposed to their own interests?
- Did they fulfil the company's expectations?
- Did they understand the counterparty's needs?
- What kind of relationship did they build with the other party?
- Did they create value?
- Were they able to adapt to change?

Attributing the points will allow you to identify what is bad and needs more work versus what is good. A score below 20 suggests that the negotiator requires training and/or additional guidance. As you might have noticed, the assessment of performance may be difficult to quantify precisely. When the review is carried out, it is important to keep in mind the subjective nature of the exercise. Errors are usually easier to spot than the things that are done well. Here are the most common mistakes that negotiators make which can hinder the closing of the deal:

- unilateral focus – neglecting the other side's needs;
- letting price out-shadow other interests;
- letting oneself be driven by ego;
- tunnel vision – failure to see beyond the positions;
- knife on the throat approach – neglecting alternatives and creative options;
- ineffective communication skills;

- good strategist armed with poor people skills;
- searching too hard for common ground to accommodate the relationship.

There should also be a benchmark against which you evaluate the results of the negotiation process. It makes sense to assess performance in relation to the assumptions that were made in the preparation phase. With this in mind, you can use the Preparation Matrix that you will find at the end of this book as a reference tool for a full scope review. The Negotiation Evaluation Checklist is a nutshell version of the main questions that relate back to the Preparation Matrix.

Negotiation Evaluation Checklist

- Is the mission statement mirrored in the outcome? Is the answer to the *How will we win?* question consistent with how you actually won?
- Did you manage to achieve the goal you set?
- Has the objective captured by the *What for?* question been fulfilled?
- Is the deal within the maximum and minimum target (and not below the walk away point)?
- Has the decision about closing been made based on the accurate assessment of all the available information?
- Is the outcome better than your BATNA?
- Will the relationship with the other party following the negotiation be strengthened?
- Does the deal add value (tangible and intangible)?
- Is the deal implementable?
- Does the agreement create a healthy negotiation culture?
- What lessons can you apply from the past negotiation to improve your (and/or your team's) performance next time?

How to move forward post negotiation

Stay focused – the deal being closed doesn't mean that it's the end. If not yet done, after the closing you should formalise the content of the agreement and prepare a contract. The degree of formality of the paperwork may differ depending on the type of deal, the relationship between the parties (especially the level of trust) as well as the culture. It is important that you understand the context properly.

I recall one of my mandates for a negotiation training at a large multinational company with its offices in Eastern Europe. In the course of negotiating the scope of the assignment, I was presented with a 27-page contract for a two-day workshop. My first impression was that the client does not trust me and is trying to protect their intellectual property from an external consultant. This made my negotiation approach a bit reserved. We spent a considerable amount of time negotiating the terms of the contract, while it would have been more beneficial to invest this energy into discussing the training content. What I failed to understand back then was that the client was from a very formal and risk-averse culture. A detailed contract was their standard way of doing business. My misunderstanding of the culture surely made me less effective (and less relationship-oriented) in that particular negotiation. The lesson here is to not hesitate to admit when you don't understand something that the other party wants.

The next thing you will need to do is set clear milestones with a timescale for the execution of the deal. During the negotiation time is on your side and there is value in taking things slow and having patience. The dynamic changes post negotiation. After the closing, time can be an enemy. People can get stuck in a different paradigm. Once the deal is closed, the energy levels tend to go down. Some negotiators slip into reactive mode. This is a mistake. You need to make sure to keep the momentum going. Don't let things go stale or lose their way.

The same reversed dynamic applies to flexibility. During the negotiation, the winds can change direction and you need to be able to adapt accordingly. Post negotiation, the level of flexibility should be reduced. You need to remain firm in what was agreed.

To manage the time in an efficient manner, it is recommended to define who does what and by when (the three Ws – who, what, when). Lack of clear task distribution is a hindering factor to implementing the deal. In order to avoid this, you should identify the key players in transitioning and implementing the agreement.

Another difference between the negotiation itself and the post negotiation reality is that it is more difficult to control the number of people who will be involved in the implementation of the deal. Make sure that when decisions are made after the deal is closed, it includes all stakeholders.

To clear the way of any obstacles to implementation, educate any new participants in your expectations. Both parties should have the same expectations so that no one is deceived.

The importance of maintaining the task and relationship balance remains unchanged. Make sure to cultivate good relations by maintaining engagement with key negotiation partners as a focal point for success.

Remember to always be positive – before, during and after the negotiation. Your mindset combined with a strategic approach is the recipe for success. Celebrate your achievement, individually and with your negotiation partner. By rewarding yourself for past performance, you will be more motivated for future endeavours. High-Impact negotiations consume a lot of effort and mental energy. Why not take a holiday to recharge before the next big one?

Negotiation Relationship Management (NRM)

Since negotiation is a human-to-human interaction, it is vital to keep the momentum going in that sphere too. A positive dynamic up until the end is a golden bridge to future negotiations. Here are a few tips on how you can cement the relationship post negotiation.

- Introduce **bonding rituals** that only you and your negotiation partner know about. For example, Harvey and Donna in the Netflix series *Suits* had the 'can opener ritual' that they performed whenever they had something big to celebrate. The viewer never found out what that ritual was, which was exactly the point. The sense of sharing a secret makes the bonding experience more exclusive.

- Keep a **record of important dates** – anniversaries, birthdays and other meaningful events for your negotiation partner. Send them wishes on these occasions. Harvey Mackay, the renowned American businessman and author, recommends using the good old Rolodex (a file for holding names, contact details and notes in the format of cards attached horizontally to a cylinder that rotates as you flip through it). If you prefer an electronic organiser, there are plenty of digital applications available for downloading.

- Send **personalised messages**, preferably handwritten or at least hand-signed. A short thank you letter sent by post shows the additional efforts you underwent to let your negotiation partner know that you appreciate them. Few people send a thank you message at all, which makes receiving one the more valuable.

- Find out what your negotiation partner likes and send them **a small gift** that caters to those tastes. It does not have to be, nor should it be, anything expensive because this may make them uncomfortable and in some legal systems be considered as bribery. Instead, the gift should be thought through and original. The point is to make it personalised and memorable.

- Invite your negotiation partner and their team out for a nice **celebratory meal**. Choose an exceptional place in a nice location, with excellent food and corresponding service. Needless to say, take care of the bill without splitting the costs. Be discrete and avoid showing them the final check amount. Most high-end restaurants have 'lady menus' – menu cards that do not display the meal prices. You may call in advance when you make reservations and arrange to have such menus for your guests.

- On the strategic level, you might want to **grant a lightweight demand** to your negotiation partner should there still be any pending asks at their end after the closing. Word of caution: this should be the lowest weight concession for you, and it should be made known to the other party that this is an exceptional gesture of courtesy.

Bonding – the glue that keeps it all together

During the negotiation, the negotiator plays an active role as the master of the ceremony (MC). Post-negotiation their part slightly changes. The function of the negotiator is now to be a secure base. Their main focus should be on creating trust to drive the process forward. This is done through bonding.

The cycle of bonding encompasses three phases, as shown in Figure 14.1. When two parties start the negotiation, they enter into a system of interdependency – they need each other to reach their individual objectives. This is how a bond is initially formed. If the negotiation is executed with equal regard to both the task and the relation, the bond between the parties will be strengthened. When the process comes to an end (the parties reach an agreement or agree to no agreement), there is the moment of separation. Any ending brings along a feeling of loss due to the change in circumstances. This causes grief.

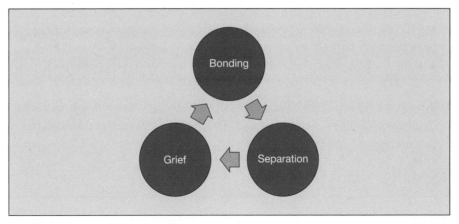

Figure 14.1 The cycle of bonding

Although to grieve after the old order is a natural psychological reaction, few business professionals embrace this emotion. It is not seen as 'professional'. Ignoring the grief phase after the negotiation can cause serious damage both to the task implementation as well as to the relationship between the parties. Keeping momentum post negotiation should include a bit of space for mentally embracing the loss of what was (the pre-negotiation reality and the negotiation process itself) and the transition to a new beginning.

Expert view

Agent Gary Noesner
Chief, FBI Crisis Negotiation Unit (retired)

Essentially, everything in life is based on relationships – the personal sphere, work and when dealing with conflict. If we want to influence the other party, it is absolutely essential that we first build a relationship with them. To establish a relationship, we need to have a bond. Trust is a fundamental element. The starting point is listening. It is an active endeavour. Listening consists of showing attentiveness to the other party's needs, acknowledging their point of view (this does not implicate agreeing), demonstrating interest about wanting to learn more, and labelling emotions. People essentially want to be listened to, understood and appreciated.

Everyone wants to be treated with respect and dignity. One of the key factors is likeability. The things that make someone engaging, genuine and understanding are the essence of likeability. It causes people to want to cooperate and avoid conflict escalation. Even when challenges or differences of opinion occur, we are more open to the other's point of view if we have the likeability established, and we made the other person feel listened to. You should leave people with the impression that what they have to say is important.

Among the FBI negotiators, the process of trust building and bonding is referred to as 'the behavioural change stairway'. The point is not to get right down to the problem solving. It is not recommended to propose ready-made solutions. You need to earn the right to do that. Take time to create the relationship first, then work on the issue.

Keeping the momentum after a negotiation without a deal

The above tips and techniques for keeping the momentum relate to the scenario when the deal was closed. The question that now needs to be addressed is what to do if there is no agreement, which is a perfectly valid option. Your focus in this case is twofold: internal and external.

First of all, do not panic and do not start doubting your negotiation capacity. Treat the past negotiation as a learning lesson, not as an attack on your skills. Do an internal post-mortem. Ask yourself what happened and what could have been done differently – on the strategic level, in the relation with the other party and in terms of your own negotiation attitude. You can use the Cher turn-back-time technique we discovered in Chapter 1.

Once the post-mortem is done, look at the bright side to create psychological leverage for the future. The way that you bounce back post negotiation determines your future performance. If you allow lack of closure to chip away at your confidence, you are going to create a self-fulfilling prophecy. It is better to keep practicing your negotiation skills instead.

On the external level, the focus on actively preserving the relationship will be milder, but you should not completely neglect your negotiation partner. Continue the relationship no matter the outcome. You meet people twice in life – once when you climb up the ladder and once when you descend from it. Send the other party a message thanking them for the joint process and their efforts.

Be specific what you appreciated about the interaction with them. This shows that you paid attention and genuinely value them.

You can also ask for their honest feedback on your performance. This will allow you to identify areas for future improvement. Keep an open ear when you listen to their criticism. Not everything might have gone well, so be prepared for their need to vent the frustration. Do not counterattack or provide arguments in defence of yourself. Just listen, digest and improve. If possible, ask for referrals. This might open doors to future business opportunities.

The most important factor is to keep the communication with the other party alive. You never know where that may lead to in the future. Ask if it would be acceptable that you contact them again should another opportunity surface. As a general rule, people prefer to do business with others whom they already know and whom they feel they can trust. Your goal is relationship retention and loyalty of your negotiation partner. Be a farmer, not a hunter – sustain and cultivate the negotiation relation.

It is vital that you maintain a client for life approach. Keep any promises that you might have made during the negotiation. Over-delivering is a great way to strengthen the relationship. Few go to the additional effort post negotiation; this is something that you can distinguish yourself with. Let your elegant attitude and high professional standards be your personal negotiation brand.

Summary of key take-aways

1 Evaluation of the results should include a strategic check combined with a review of performance of the negotiator.

2 Do not lose sight of your objective after the negotiation – the deal being closed doesn't mean that it's the end.

3 Keep the flame alive on the relational level through Negotiation Relationship Management (NRM).

4 Leave a bit of space for mentally embracing the loss of what was before making the transition to a new beginning.

5 Let your classy behaviour and high professional standards be the reason for others to want to engage in future deal-making with you.

Further reading

1   10 tips before, during and after you negotiate. 2021. QBE See https://www. qbe.com/au/brokers/support/q-nect/knowledge/negotiation-tips.

2   Hamza-Goodacre, D., Jefford, S. and Simister, N. (2013) Supporting international climate negotiators: a monitoring and evaluation framework. Climate and Development Knowledge Network. November 2013.

3   Honig, A. (2010) *You Closed the Deal, Now What? 6 Things to Do After the Sale.* Customer Think. See https://customerthink.com/you-closed-the-deal-now-what-6-things-to-do-after-the-sale.

4   How to manage customer relationships after closing deals. 2019. Freshdesk Blog. See https://freshdesk.com/customer-experience/manage-customer-relationships-after-closing-deals-blog/

5   O'Hara, C. (2016) How to bounce back after a failed negotiation. *Harvard Business Review.* See https://hbr.org/2016/04/how-to-bounce-back-after-a-failed-negotiation

6   Patel, N. (2015) *How to Win Your Negotiation While Preserving Good Relationships.* Forbes.

SUMMARY

High-impact negotiations are a specific breed, be it in the professional sphere or beyond. The higher the stakes, the greater the emotions involved. In these types of transactions, aligning a clear strategic objective with relational aspects is the key to success. A high-impact negotiation starts in the mind of the negotiator – with what they perceive as important for them or the party they represent. The mindset that this attitude creates can make or break the deal.

Therefore, a prerequisite to the strategic design of the negotiation process is the ability to manage oneself – the fears, hopes and aspirations that you bring to the table. No amount of tactics nor toolbox can replace a genuine belief in one's negotiation power. Sadly, faith alone is not sufficient either. Confidence comes from mastery of the process. There is value in focusing on yourself first, your preparation and self-control. This is the aim of this Guide – to first instill the right negotiation mindset and then to assist you through the steps of the negotiation process: defining what you want, organising the negotiation team, setting expectations and limits to what you can and cannot do and making the best use of time.

A winner's mindset on the personal level is equivalent to the negotiation mission on the strategic level. The purpose of a mission is to announce exactly where you are heading. It serves as a compass for those behaviours and actions that will help get you there. As such, the mission statement creates a certain negotiation culture that can distinguish you and your firm from competition. Setting the goal – the implementation of a concrete plan to fulfil the mission, establishing the objective, setting the target, and deciding on the best approach are strategic tools for the execution of the mission.

Successfully executing a high-stakes negotiation also involves understanding the outcomes (monetary and non-financial) you could face from various options and how to best optimise them to fulfil your negotiation mission. When parties enter the negotiation, it is because they each need a piece of the jigsaw to achieve their individual goals. Otherwise, there would be no negotiation. As long as there is communication, there is an interest. Your task is to identify what the other party needs and how you can solve their situation, while also securing your objectives.

Negotiation is not just a process, but a human-to-human interaction. It is essential to understand what constitutes value to the other party and how creating value might translate into a deal that is seen as positive by both parties, and one that is beneficial to all. In high-stakes negotiations, a win–win should be understood as being part of something bigger than just securing a unilateral victory. If you discover your own and the other parties' needs, then you can use them to come to a good outcome. Therefore, in a way you are using the goals of both parties to get what you want – this is where internal alignment is bridged with the external negotiation with the other party, and the task and relationship aspects come together. Of course, there is always the possibility that despite doing everything right, you may not win the deal. No agreement is not equivalent to a disagreement. A graceful exit is at times better than a suboptimal close.

Your negotiation style and approach are your personal (and/or organisational) brand. The way that you design the right environment, take the lead by opening the negotiation, by executing the dealing phase and by closing are the true marks of an effective negotiator. Elegance and class during and after the process are more than courtesies towards the other party, they are gifts for yourself that go beyond the negotiation arena.

Time to get started. Practice makes perfect and preparation is key but remember to be open to directional change throughout the process as long as the goal remains clear. Uncertainty is always present in real life and course corrections take place as winds change direction. Take advantage of this roadmap that allows for proactive flexibility and be open to creative solutions. I wish you many successful and enriching negotiations.

COMPENDIUM OF KEY TAKE-AWAYS

Chapter 1: Negotiation starts from within

1 The most important negotiator you have to win over is you.

2 A negotiation is a human-to-human interaction.

3 Negotiation challenges are universal; chances are you and the other negotiator shares the same ones.

4 You have control over your psyche and only you can claim your negotiation power.

5 Focus on your strengths, and do not allow your challenges to hold you back.

Chapter 2: Defining the negotiation mission statement

1 Omission of a clearly defined negotiation mission is a strategic disadvantage.

2 The purpose of a mission is to announce exactly where you are heading, both internally and externally, in the high-stakes negotiation.

3 Values depict those behaviours and actions that will help get you there.

4 Start by answering the question: *How will we win?*

5 Ensure that the mission and values support each other.

Chapter 3: Setting the goal

1 A goal is a broad statement of where you want to end up; targets help measure the extent to which you achieved your end state.

2 Do not enter in a negotiation without knowing what your goal is.

3 The goal should address both the task and the relationship-orientation (T + R).

4 Set challenging goals for yourself; however, once you obtain them, do not make the other party feel like a loser.

5 Be ready to re-evaluate your goals and walk away if the context changes to the extent that your overall goal cannot be met.

Chapter 4: Establishing the objective

1 A negotiation objective identifies the purpose of the negotiation goal.

2 Use the *What for?* question to test your motives.

3 Prepare a set of parameters for your objective.

4 Distinguish the supporting parameters and eliminate those that do not serve your objective.

5 Build a bridge between your objectives and the objectives of the other party to create commitment to the end goal.

Chapter 5: Gathering the necessary information

1 Equip yourself with all the necessary information before starting the negotiation.

2 Collect the data on two levels: environment-oriented and person-centred.

3 Apply the asking–listening–verifying approach to information gathering.

4 Check the accuracy of the assumptions you made in the course of information gathering.

5 Find out what is important to the other party and design an environment where they need something from you.

Chapter 6: Deciding the best approach for the negotiation

1 The choice of strategy is a balancing act between the task and the relationship.

2   Tailor the strategy to your desired output.

3   For long-term partnerships, apply the collaborative approach.

4   Follow the hybrid path: competition–avoidance–accommodation–compromise–collaboration.

5   You do not need to compromise the relationship to reach your objectives.

Chapter 7: Negotiating virtually

1   Virtual negotiation is nothing more than a shift of perspective with a strategic e-design.

2   When direct human contact is limited, the relational aspect needs to be even more strongly addressed in the negotiation process.

3   There is a richness of virtual tools to choose from. Use them to navigate the e-negotiation arena with more ease.

4   Minimise any potential sources of digital distractions.

5   Adapt the medium to negotiator preferences and the effect that you want to make.

Chapter 8: Designing the right environment for the negotiation

1   Align strategic preparation with a positive attitude.

2   Create the three grand negotiation illusions: autonomy and choice, ownership and victory.

3   In a high-stakes negotiation, the more uncomfortable it is on the inside, the more agreeable you should make it on the outside.

4   Be the host both for the process, for yourself and for the other party.

5   Create a relationship of trust and engage the other party in a genuine, sincere, and honest manner.

Chapter 9: Creating value in negotiations

1   Value adding is the standard; value creating is the premium.

2   Creating value in negotiations starts by changing the I-focus.

3   A long-lasting and valuable agreement is one where the objectives are reached, and the relationship between the parties is strengthened. Make sure you invest in the relation.

4   Look for the external value outside of the direct scope of your negotiation with the other party.

5   You increase your value to the other party when you make them believe that you have alternatives and can create options for them.

Chapter 10: Taking the lead in the negotiation

1   Negotiation is a combination of management and leadership skills.

2   Projecting somewhat limited power (the Miss Marple approach) is more useful than engaging in a power struggle.

3   Exercising power without building a robust relationship will not lead to an executable agreement.

4   A great negotiator-leader is someone who the other party wants to willingly follow.

5   Deciding on the roles involves strategic planning and finding a psychological fit.

Chapter 11: Opening the negotiation

1   The opening is a critical moment for establishing your position, building rapport with the other party and taking the lead in the process.

2   Be aware that the anchoring effect might impact your own perception.

3   You can craft an anchor and use it to strengthen the allure of your offering.

4   In deciding whether to open first use the following rule: If the stakes are fairly low for you, and to test how the other side values you, allow them to open first.

5   Be the one who designs, proposes and manages the agenda.

Chapter 12: Successfully executing the dealing phase

1   Agree on the process before you introduce the demands.

2   Present your demands first, then listen to the list of the other party.

3   Prepare a hierarchy of demands and categorise them according to heavy-, middle- and lightweight and do not omit the non-negotiable items.

4   Be careful how you word your demands.

5   Uncover the hidden interests behind the demands.

Chapter 13: Closing the deal

1   Negotiation is concluded when the negotiated terms can be implemented and there is a potential for a lasting business relationship between the parties.

2   Both agreement and no agreement are valid ways of ending a negotiation.

3   Compare the expected costs and benefits to see if closing makes sense.

4   In case of a tie between pragmatism and ego after performing a cost–benefit analysis, pragmatism should win.

5   Do not allow the end on the horizon and the temptation to close the deal to blur your judgement of the issues that can surface in the last rounds.

Chapter 14: Keeping the momentum after the negotiation

1   Evaluation of the results should include a strategic check combined with a review of performance of the negotiator.

2   Do not lose sight of your objective after the negotiation – the deal being closed doesn't mean that it's the end.

3   Keep the flame alive on the relational level through Negotiation Relationship Management (NRM).

4   Leave a bit of space for mentally embracing the loss of what was before making the transition to a new beginning.

5   Let your classy behaviour and high professional standards be the reason for others to want to engage in future deal-making with you.

PREPARATION MATRIX[4]

The preparation matrix is a legacy for your upcoming negotiations. It is a user-friendly framework which covers all the steps, phases and elements of the negotiation process, along with a break-down indication of what to pay attention to before, during and after the negotiation. The matrix serves as a tool for preparation, evaluating and monitoring progress. The time you invest in filling it in will help you reap benefits during the negotiation by helping you stay on track of what you set out to achieve.

1 Three-level preparation:

   (a) you (self-management)

   (b) strategic

   (c) relational

2 Defining the mission statement – *How will we win?*

3 Setting the goal – implementation of a concrete plan to fulfil the mission

4 Establishing the objective – *What for?*

5 Setting the target (max and min)

6 Information gathering and profiling of your partner

7 Choice of strategy:

   (a) Competition

   (b) Compromise

   (c) Avoidance

   (d) Accommodation

   (e) Collaboration

   (f) Hybrid

8 Leadership – distribution of team roles

9 Creating the right environment

---

[4] Adapted from Negotiation Booster

10 Agenda setting

11 Opening offer (ZOPA, Anchoring)

12 Demands (categorisation and hierarchy of importance)

13 Identification of interests vs positions

14 BATNA (outside the negotiation) – perpetual effort (before, during and after)

15 Options (inside the negotiation)

16 Communication (verbal, non-verbal, para-verbal, virtual)

17 Closing and execution

The preparation matrix blueprint

Before the negotiation	During the negotiation	After the negotiation
1		
2		
3		
4		
5		
6 gathering of information	6 verifying accuracy of the information	
7 assumption regarding which strategy to use	7 + adaptation according to their willingness to cooperate	
8	8 leading the negotiation	
9 preparing the scene	9 creating the right atmosphere during the negotiation	9 keeping the flame alive after through Negotiation Relationship Management (NRM)
10 agenda preparation	10 agenda presentation	
11 prepare opening offer	11 present opening offer	
12 demands preparation	12 demands presentation	
	13	
14	14	14
15 internally (what options do you have)	15 externally, with the other party (what options do you have together)	
16	16	16
	17 closing	17 execution

GLOSSARY OF NEGOTIATION TERMS

Accommodation – referred to as yielding or *lose–win*, an approach that places the relationship first while one's own needs are not satisfied. The level of cooperation is high, but assertiveness is low. A prevalent behavioural pattern exercised in families or between romantic partners.

Anchoring – the limits set forth by the opening offer, which will serve as a reference point around which the other party will structure their offer. Strong signal of expectations and standards.

Anticipatory emotions – the imaginary emotions of how it would feel having already achieved something, used as a motivational tool to boost the chances of obtaining a desired result or spurring to action.

Avoidance – a *lose–lose* negotiation approach synonymous with delay or not taking action. Mediocre both in the level of cooperation between the parties and in the level of individual assertiveness.

BATNA (best alternative to a negotiated agreement) – the fallback position when an agreement in a specific situation or with a particular partner cannot be reached, outside of the negotiation (as opposed to options, which are inside the negotiation).

Boomerang effect – a negative effect of an inadequate opening offer, when the negotiation partner considers the offer as too high and throws back an equally outrageous offer for the sake of reciprocity. The parties risk entering into an ego struggle, which will divert attention from the task.

Chilling effect – a negative effect of an inadequate opening offer, which causes the counterpart to lose interest in the negotiation at the outset. Their perception is that the negotiation is not in good faith.

Collaboration – a principled approach to negotiation that balances the task and relationship. Synonymous with the popular phrase *win–win*. Centred on finding an agreement that is efficient in the distribution of the resource, is fair to both sides, and reinforces the relationship between them. Involves identifying the interests behind the positions and determining which needs are fixed and which are flexible, and then crafting creative options to bridge those needs.

Competition – one of the negotiation strategies based on power, referred to as the *win–lose* approach. Characterised by forceful behaviour, stating demands instead of investigating mutual interests, reluctance to making concessions and insistence on the satisfaction of one's own needs.

Compromise – the *win–lose* and *lose–win* approach to negotiation because both parties gain and both lose something. An easy and fast means of distribution of a limited resource by splitting it in half, which does not require too much time or creative effort. An approach that does not maximise the benefits of the resource.

Concession – something that one party gives up in exchange for something else in response to a demand of the other party. The conceding party should exchange a good of less value for a good of higher value.

Counterpart – a noun used to depict the other party at the negotiation table, a label that might lead to a more competitive and aggressive negotiation dynamic.

Deadlock – a situation reached by the negotiation parties, in which each is waiting for the other one to make a move, and they find it difficult to progress. May happen when the parties get stuck in their rigid positions. Requires unblocking or abandoning the negotiation.

Demands – the tokens of trade in a negotiation, which constitute the negotiation mass; should be listed in order of importance and be used for making concessions.

Ego-tiation – the process of negotiation driven by an inordinate need for recognition and approval, dominated by one's ego.

Emotional balcony – a place in your mind that you retreat to in order to gain an objective outlook on the negotiation, where you are the spectator and not the actor, a place where you can manage your emotions and take time for rational decision-making.

Framing – structuring the dynamic to serve one's objective by limiting the options of the other negotiator. Giving a choice within controlled limits, for example, asking the other party which ink they will sign the contract in, blue or black. The choice is theirs, but the only option is signing the contract.

Hybrid approach – a mix between the other five negotiation approaches (competition, collaboration, avoidance, accommodation and compromise), tailored to the type of negotiation partner, the negotiation goal, the negotiation dynamic and the situational context.

Impasse – a situation when the parties cannot reach an agreement, equivalent to a deadlock.

Impression management – an attempt to control or alter the impression one makes.

Interests (motives) – the underlying factors behind the position, the reasons why one wants something. See: principal interests.

Master negotiator – a negotiator who has mastery of the tools of negotiation and self-empowerment.

Mental map – an inner global positioning system (GPS) consisting of life experiences, culture, education, upbringing, and family traditions that influences how an individual perceives the world and that drives their behaviour.

Mirror negotiation – the image you display in terms of self-assurance, inner status and authority that is reflected in the actions of your counterpart and ultimately affects their negotiation approach towards you.

Needs – a continuum of elements that stimulate behaviour. According to Maslow's hierarchy of needs, there are five levels of needs: physiological, safety, belonging, esteem and self-actualisation.

Negotiation – a process of perceptual self-management during which two parties with common and opposing needs and interests try to reach a mutually acceptable agreement, which harnesses the needs and interests of both sides. Ideally, a process driven by reason rather than ego or emotions. A negotiation consists of two elements – task and relationship – and is driven by scarcity of resources.

Negotiation Booster – a synergetic approach that leverages the task-related aspects of a negotiation with the underlying emotional factors. A self-management toolkit designed to tame emotions, ego and stress by means of personal empowerment.

Negotiation partner – a noun used to depict the other party at the negotiation table, a label that might help shape a more cooperative negotiation dynamic.

Negotiator – a person with the necessary skillset and training to conduct a negotiation. An individual who sees the big picture (the experts will take care of the details), who can control their emotions, bridge the task and relationship aspects of the negotiation, and execute the negotiation strategy.

Objective – what you want to achieve in a negotiation.

Opening offer – the first offer put on the table in a negotiation, which creates a lasting impression. Should be as close as possible to the other party's barely acceptable terms. See: anchoring.

Opponent – a noun used to depict the other party at the negotiation table, a strong label that might lead to a competitive and aggressive negotiation dynamic.

Options – creative solutions introduced when there is no ZOPA, but the parties still want to reach an agreement. Options are inside the negotiation, as opposed to BATNA.

Partnership – an arrangement between two parties that bridges the task and the relationship aspects in view of a long-term cooperation.

Para-verbal communication – one of the three types of communication (the other two being verbal and non-verbal), depicting how things are expressed: tone, pitch of voice, speed, pace, pauses.

Paradigm – the lens through which you see the world.

Perception – the identification, organisation and interpretation of information that forms the way in which we understand the environment.

Position – the *what do you want* part of the negotiation dynamic. See: interests (motives).

Priming – a form of mental stimulation and thought direction where a stimulus impacts a reaction and can lead to a desired behaviour.

Reciprocity principle – the tendency for people to treat others the way they are treated.

Reinforcement principle – unambiguous, immediate and clear setting of expectations and standards of conduct that reinforces the desired behaviour.

Reservation point – the minimum one is willing to accept before walking away from the negotiation table.

Similarity principle – the urge to find a point of similarity that is deeply rooted in human psyche and that brings negotiation parties closer.

Strategy – a combination of power and cooperation that leads to the negotiation objective.

Tactics – the tools one uses to implement the negotiation strategy. They vary depending on the situational context, the type of negotiation and the other negotiator.

Tells – a term used in poker when one of the players gives off a signal that unveils how good their cards are. In the negotiation context, tells are signs conveyed by body language that are picked up on by the other party.

Tunnel vision – concentrating only on the problem, failure to see the big picture and creative solutions or alternative courses of action.

Virtual negotiation – an exchange between two parties who are trying to reach an agreement without face-to-face interaction. Can take the form of text-based (instant messaging or e-mail) or voice-based (telephone, videoconference) mode.

Window of Opportunity (WoO) – a favourable opportunity or moment to enter the negotiation, the right place and time to make an opening offer or a demand to a receptive party.

ZOPA (Zone of Possible Agreement) – numerical representation of the overlap between the most that the buyer is willing to pay and the minimum that the seller is willing to accept.

SUGGESTED FURTHER READING

Adams, Scott (2019) *Loserthink. How Untrained Brains Are Ruining the World.* New York: Portfolio/Penguin.

Adams, Scott (2017) *Win Bigly. Persuasion in a World Where Facts Don't Matter.* New York: Portfolio/Penguin.

Annis, Barbara and Gray, John (2013) *Work with Me. How Gender Intelligence Can Help You Succeed at Work and in Life.* London: Piatkus.

Barker, Alan (2016) *Improve Your Communication Skills.* New York: Kogan Page Limited.

Bergreen, Laurence (2016) *Casanova. The World of a Seductive Genius.* New York: Simon & Schuster.

Brett, Jeanne M. (2014) *Negotiating Globally. How to Negotiate Deals, Resolve Disputes, and Make Decisions Across Cultural Boundaries.* San Francisco: Jossey-Bass.

Brzezinski, Mika (2018) *Know Your Value: Women, Money and Getting What You're Worth.* Revised Edition. Hachette Books.

Burg, Bob and Mann, John David (2018) *The Go-Giver Influencer. A Little Story About a Most Persuasive Idea.* New York: Portfolio/Penguin.

Cambria, J. (2019) Parliamone. L'ascolto, l'empatia, le parole giuste per negoziare con successo in qualunque situazion. ROI Edizioni srl.

Carnegie, Dale (2006) *How to Win Friends and Influence People.* London: Vermilion.

Chu, Chin-Ning (2010) *The Art of War for Women: It's about the Art, not the War.* New York: Broadway Books.

Cialdini, Robert (2016) *Pre-Suasion. A Revolutionary Way to Influence and Persuade.* London: Random House Books.

Cicero, Marcus Tullius (2016) *How to Win an Argument. An Ancient Guide to the Art of Persuasion* (selected, edited and translated by James M. May). Princeton: Princeton University Press.

Cuddy, Amy (2016) *Presence. Bringing Your Boldest Self to Your Biggest Challenges.* London: Orion.

De Beauvoir, Simone (2011) *The Second Sex.* London: Vintage.

Dispenza, Joe (2014) *You Are the Placebo. Making Your Mind Matter.* London: Hay House UK Ltd.

Duhigg, Charles (2014) *The Power of Habit. Why We Do What We Do in Life and in Business.* New York: Random House Trade Paperbacks.

Dutton, Kevin (2011) *Flipnosis. The Art of Split-Second Persuasion.* London: Arrow Books.

Eger, Edith (2017) *The Choice. Even in Hell Hope can Flower.* London: Rider.

Fleming, Kerrie (2016) *The Leader's Guide to Emotional Agility. How to Use Soft Skills to Get Hard Results.* Harlow: Pearson Education Limited.

Freud, Sigmund (1922) *Group Psychology and the Analysis of the Ego.* Vienna: The International Psycho-Analytical Press.

Gino, Francesca (2019) *Rebel Talent. Why it Pays to Break the Rules at Work and in Life.* London: Pan Books.

Greene, Robert (1998) *The 48 Laws of Power.* London: Profile Books Ltd.

Greene, Robert (2001) *The Art of Seduction.* New York: Penguin Books.

Harkiolakis, Nicholas, Halkias, Daphne and Abadir, Sam (2016) *e-Nogotiations. Networking and Cross-Cultural Business Transactions.* New York: Routledge.

Heinrichs, Jay (2017) *Thank You for Arguing. What Cicero, Shakespeare and the Simpsons Can Teach Us About the Art of Persuasion.* London: Penguin Random House UK.

Hill, Napoleon (2005) *Think and Grow Rich.* New York: Jeremy P. Tarcher/Penguin.

Hofstede, Geert (2001) *Culture's Consequences: Comparing Values, Behaviors, Institutions, and Organizations Across Nations.* Second Edition. California: Sage Publications.

Holiday, Ryan (2016) *Ego is the Enemy. The Fight to Master Our Greatest Opponent.* London: Profile Books Ltd.

Jagodzinska, Katarzyna (2016) Egotiation is the new negotiation: the concept of negotiation revisited. *Eurasian Journal of Business and Management* 4 (2): 72–80. Accessed 30 May 2020. DOI: 10.15604/ejss.2016.04.02.007

Jagodzinska, Katarzyna (2016) How to manage perception to win negotiations. *International Journal of Social Science Studies* 4 (2): 69–77. Accessed 30 May 2020. DOI: 10.11114/ijsss.v4i2.1320

Jang, Jia (2015) *Rejection Proof. How to Beat Fear and Become Invincible.* London: Random House.

Johnson, Spencer (1999) *Who Moved My Cheese? An Amazing Way to Deal with Change in Your Work and in Your Life.* London: Vermilion.

Jung, Carl G. (1968) *Man and His Symbols.* USA: Dell Publishing.

Kelly, Megyn (2016) *Settle for More.* New York: Harpers Collins Publishers.

Machiavelli, Niccolo (2011) *The Prince.* UK: Penguin Random House.

Mackay, Harvey (1997) *Dig Your Well Before You're Thirsty.* New York: Currency Doubleday.

Mandela, Ndaba (2018) *11 Life Lessons from Nelson Mandela.* London: Windmill Books.

Manzoni, Jean-François and Barsoux, Jean-Louis (2007) *The Set-Up-To-Fail Syndrome. Overcoming the Undertow of Expectations.* Boston: Harvard Business School Publishing Corporation.

Maslow, Abraham H. (1954) *Motivation and Personality.* USA: Addison-Wesley Educational Publishers Inc.

Meyer, Erin (2015) *The Culture Map: Decoding How People Think, Lead, and Get Things Done Across Cultures.* Philadelphia: PublicAffairs.

Mnookin, Robert H., Peppet, Scott R. and Tulumello, Andrew S. (2000) *Beyond Winning. Negotiating to Create Value in Deals and Disputes.* Cambridge: The Belknap Press of Harvard University Press.

Morrison, Terri, Conaway, Wayne A. and Borden, George A. (1994) *Kiss, Bow or Shake Hands.* Avon: Adams Media Corporation.

Noesner, Gary (2018) *Stalling for Time. My Life as an FBI Hostage Negotiator.* Random House USA Inc, New York, USA.

Oblinger, Dan (2018) *Life or Death Listening.* USA: Amazon Kindle Direct Publishing.

Oblinger, Dan (2019) *The 28 Laws of Listening.* USA: End of the Drive, Secondhand Ranch, Rose Hill.

Greene, Robert (2012) *Mastery.* London: Profile Books Ltd.

Sandberg, Sheryl and Grant, Adam (2017) *Option B. Facing Adversity, Building Resilience and Finding Joy.* London: WH Allen.

Sharrot, Tali (2017) *The Influential Mind. What the Brain Reveals About Our Power to Change Others.* London: Abacus.

Tzu, Sun (1988) *The Art of War.* Boulder: Shambhala Publications, Inc.

Waal, Frans De (2019) *The Age of Empathy.* London: Souvenir Press.

Ury, William (1992) *Getting Past No. Negotiating with Difficult People.* London: Century Business.

Williams, Greg and Iyer, Pat (2016) *Body Language Secrets to Win More Negotiations. How to Read any Opponent and Get What You Want.* Wayne: The Career Press Inc.

INDEX

Page numbers in *italics* denote figures.